JOEL SHAPIRO

JOEL SHAPIRO

Painted Wood Sculpture and Drawings

Interview by Ellen Phelan / edited by Amy Newman

March 24 - April 22, 1995

The Pace Gallery 32 East 57 Street New York City

PaceWildenstein

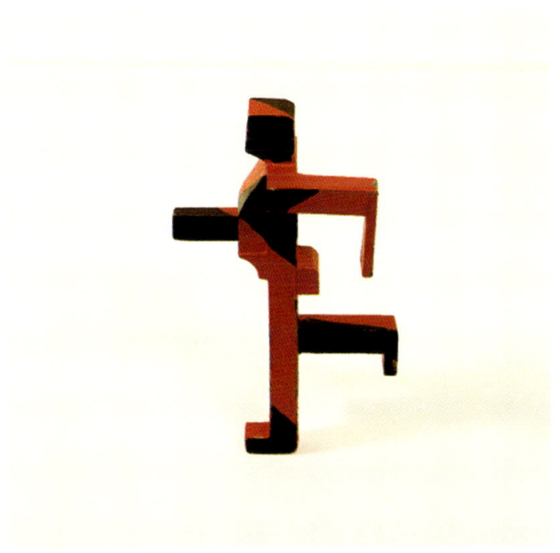

untitled, 1976-77, oil paint on bronze, 9 ¾ x 2 ⅝ x 5"

untitled, 1973, enamel on wood, 6 ½ x 6 ½ x 1 ⅛"

ELLEN:
People don't generally think of painting when they think of your work, but you've been painting sculptures on and off for quite some time.

JOEL:
Yes, intermittently since the late 1960s.

ELLEN:
The wall-mounted folded forms from the late 1970s were painted, but the first freestanding, painted piece that I remember was the small bronze running man [shown at the Whitney in 1977]. You somehow projected light onto the piece, and were painting shadows—which implied a fixed light source.

JOEL:
Right. I used a klieg light because it was an intense source of light that I could control, that I could crop to create a pattern on the piece. I wanted the pattern to originate elsewhere. I *had* painted work before that, but I was never terribly involved with *color*; I always used paint as a means of resolution, of completing the work.

ELLEN:
That was a very rationally justified way of adding paint. But it seems to me that, over time of course, your approach has gotten much more intuitive.

JOEL:
Yes. Before that, I think everything I'd painted had been monochromatic, using a layer of paint, a single color to envelope the form. So I was really more interested in the surface than in any kind of differentiation of form. Later, when I did those running figures, each one was painted differently. But the one that I showed at the Whitney had this projection which had a rational basis behind it, a certain point of view. I was using the paint topographically, to organize separate parts or to differentiate one section from another section. It was a very small piece, and then I picked ordinary colors, red and black.

ELLEN:
Exactly. I was thinking of Constructivism in the color choice. I remember both of us being quite interested in the show

that Margit Rowell had organized for the Guggenheim Museum, "The Planar Dimension"—mostly work in relief.

JOEL:
Yes, it was an interesting show—interesting because the parameters of the paint application were more determined by structure than illusion.

ELLEN:
I remember the series, around '78 or '79, of quite free, discovered, organic shapes. They were gouache drawings, works on paper, that seemed to have a direct analogue in a series of painted wall reliefs. That's a very under-known aspect of your work.

JOEL:
I spent about two years doing gouaches and painting reliefs simultaneously. But although I had a show of the reliefs at the Paula Cooper Gallery in 1979, I never showed them with the gouaches.

I did other pieces, too. After the reliefs I began to paint large freestanding sculptures. Sometimes they were only partially painted—for example, the head would be painted blue, and the body remained wood. And I did other reliefs as a way to clarify the *meaning* of paint in relationship to the naturalism of wood—the conceptual aspect of paint, the kind of willful aspect of paint, the juxtaposition.

ELLEN:
Do you think that painting the wood pieces gives them more reality? What do I mean by reality? Makes them exist more in the world, in a way? In the way we experience the world?

JOEL:
I think paint makes them more abstract, and removes the material or the form—the material of the form—from its source. If you have a chunk of wood, and you cover it with paint, you're disguising the material. And you're presented with a chunk of color, or a chunk of paint. Of course we know that it's painted wood or it's painted bronze or it's painted canvas. But the fact is, it denies its materiality. It might make it a more *real* idea, or a more *realized* idea.

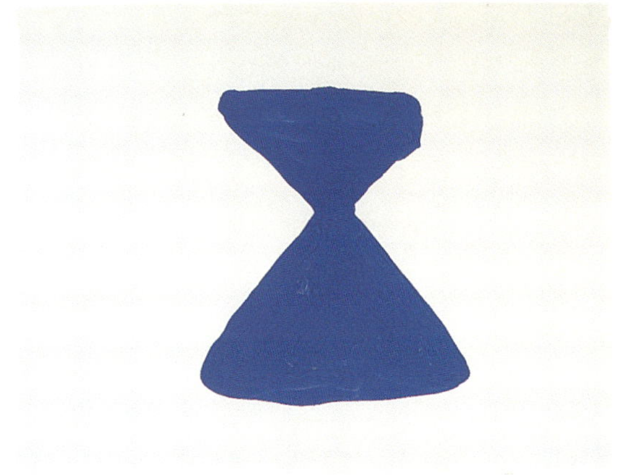

untitled, 1979, gouache on paper, 18 ⅛ x 23"

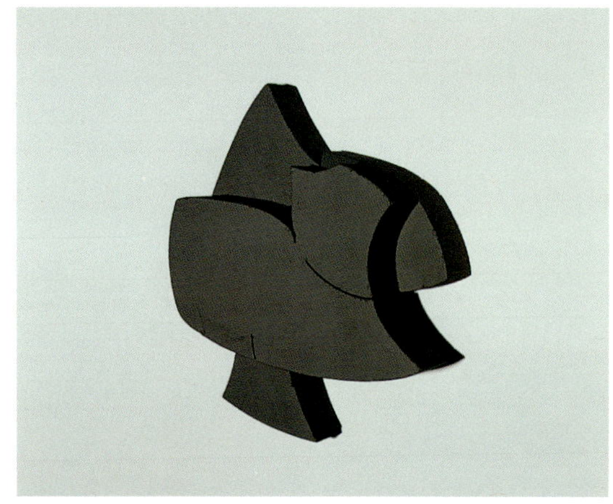

untitled, 1979-80, oil paint on wood, 9 ¼ x 7 ¾ x 3 ¹/₁₆"

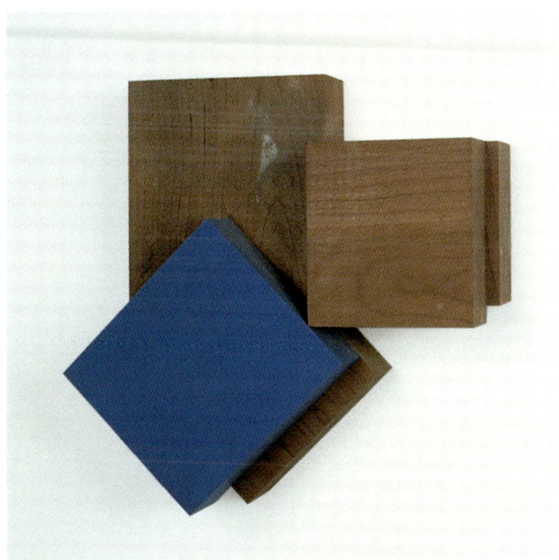

untitled, 1980, oil paint on wood, 11 ¼ x 11 ¼ x 3 ⅝"

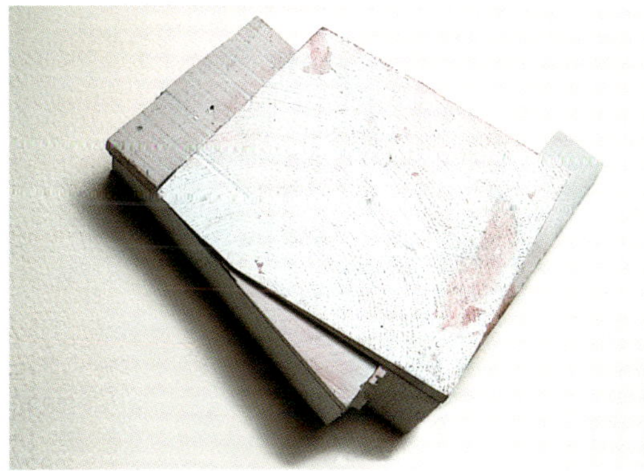

untitled, 1979, white primer on wood, 6 ½ x 8 ½ x 2 ¼"

ELLEN:
When a piece was entirely encased in color, you talked about the color being a skin that contains the form. But it's rare now that you're making a chunk of wood a color. Often, it's only one plane of a chunk of wood. Which, to me, dematerializes the chunk of wood.

JOEL:
Well yes. Depending on how thick you use the paint, you can deny the material or not deny the material.

ELLEN:
But do you deny the *monolithic* quality of the form by adding the paint?

JOEL:
I think you can reinforce it. If you look at those wall reliefs you can see that in the case of a piece made out of, say, five elements, the paint will *unify* the form. That's the opposite. But you can make the location of planes more ambiguous if you break up the surface, and *that* would deny its mass.

But what it *does* do, whether it's unifying or destroying or denying or contradicting it—is it *affects* the form. It determines how you perceive the sculpture. Solidly applied paint stops you at the surface; filmy paint creates a haze—it changes the focus. In these mahogany pieces which I have not yet painted, I've chalked certain surfaces that I intend to paint. I have a vague idea that I will accent certain aspects of the sculpture via paint. I don't know where it'll end up. Of course, the form *suggests* the paint and the color.

ELLEN:
There does seem to be a large bugaboo regarding painting sculpture in the twentieth century, or the "tradition" of modernism. Rosalind Krauss blew the whistle on Clem Greenberg for stripping the David Smith polychrome sculptures. You can think of a couple of artists who work with some kind of polychroming, but—

JOEL:
There are a considerable number of them.

ELLEN:
But I don't know if it's quite the same as what you do.

JOEL:
How about Picasso? He was a great *painter* and *sculptor*.

ELLEN:
Yes, I feel that he was a great sculptor primarily because he was a great painter. He tends to pattern up the form. Chamberlain's color—at its origins anyway—is a kind of found, *assemblage*, color. Now he does patterns on top of it. Oldenburg uses color in a mimetic fashion. He no longer seems to be much interested in an expressionist gesture that transgresses the defined or delimited form. Who else can you think of, where color is—

JOEL:
Well, in Giacometti color is very important. There are painted bronzes, painted plasters—a lot of the patinas are paint. And I think what he does is, he uses it more in terms of light and dark and shadow to amplify the form. It's very rare that he actually makes any marks, or creates some effect that denies the form. Arp painted lots of work. Archipenko—whose work I'm not all that familiar with— painted. There *is* a tradition of painting sculpture. George Sugarman. And Judd was a colorist. His approach was more radical—the color *was* the material. Quite a few peo- ple have worked in wood and paint. Because the wood is so pronounced, and so distracting. I think if you're casting in bronze, the bronze acts as a means of transforming the form from its material, from its original material. Which is a certain idea of working. That some people would object to it, requiring everything to be natural, is silly. If you're work- ing in steel, and your interest is in *steelness*, and you leave it as welded steel, fine. But I think Smith painted a lot of his steel. I'm not sure of the chronology of David Smith's paint- ed sculptures, but David Smith was a guy who was very interested in painting. In fact, the work's very *planar*. When I saw "The Age of Iron" show I was struck by how flat and contained Smith was then. It was only in the late work that he really began to cut loose. And it still seemed to me that one element was quite dependent on the prior element, one form would depend on the prior form. It always had an internal origin, rather than an external impulse.

ELLEN:

Why do you dislike the Degas *Dancer of 14 Years* with the dress on it?

JOEL:

I don't dislike it. It just never knocked me out.

ELLEN:

I ask that because, in a way, I can see paint acting like the dress. Maybe that's what I meant about "reality", more presence. Maybe it has to do with an older tradition of figurative polychrome sculptures—making it look more "real." And, so, Duane Hanson might be the end of that incredibly long line of figurative polychromism.

JOEL:

Do you mean that the literalness of the dress as description makes the material less abstract? I just think the paint is integral to the expression. And if you can achieve that with paint, or with anything, then of course the piece has more reality in some sense. It has more meaning in the world, which is what every artist strives for. It has presence and seems to be *there*. You can't just dismiss it as a pile of wood. I think the paint helps.

Yes, there is a parallel between that and the dancer, in the way that skirt kind of anchors the piece. But it's interesting, because for me, if you make something out of wood, the wood's very *real*. What you want to do is deny the wood-ness, deny its *woodiness*, so you can get involved in the meaning of the form. And I think paint can help me accomplish that in some pieces. It animates the form more, and animates the surface. It liberates it from the material.

ELLEN:

What's more interesting to me, and more singular, about the way you're painting sculpture has to do, perhaps, with the paint tending to be fairly thin. There's a kind of casualness about its use that is also *not* casual. There is a kind of gestural aspect at times. Have you thought about it very much?

JOEL:

Yes. I'm always trying to capture—at least lately—some immediacy in the work. When I make a model, and then I

make it larger, I work very hard to retain the spontaneity
of the inception of the work. And when I'm painting it I try to
do the same thing. But not all the work is so thinly painted.
Some pieces are more ponderously painted. I try to locate
what the piece is about. If it's a kind of tentative configu-
ration, it probably has a more tentative paint quality.

ELLEN:
But I think there's a kind of *economy* about the painting—
where you want the paint to *do* something. And when it
does it, you stop. That's something that I respond to, and
really like, about the way you're painting. Actually, the
works are painted very idiosyncratically, but at the same
time there's something that's very straight: that you clearly
want it to change the piece in some way. But maybe that's
not something you can plan too much ahead.

JOEL:
No. There's no planning.

ELLEN:
Right. So you try it, and if it works, great. And if it doesn't,
you do something else.

JOEL:
You wipe it off.

ELLEN:
I think that that process is quite clear in the work.

JOEL:
I don't have any preconception of painting. I'm thinking
about painting these three pieces but once I begin, what am
I thinking about? Not *doing* it. Once you start to do it,
though, the form forces a certain approach.

ELLEN:
You always ask me questions like, "What's an elated color?",
"What's a depressed color?"

JOEL:
I do believe that color can have an intrinsic metaphoric quality,
depending on how it's used, so that interests me. Not only is
it perceptual, but it has certain cultural meanings as well.

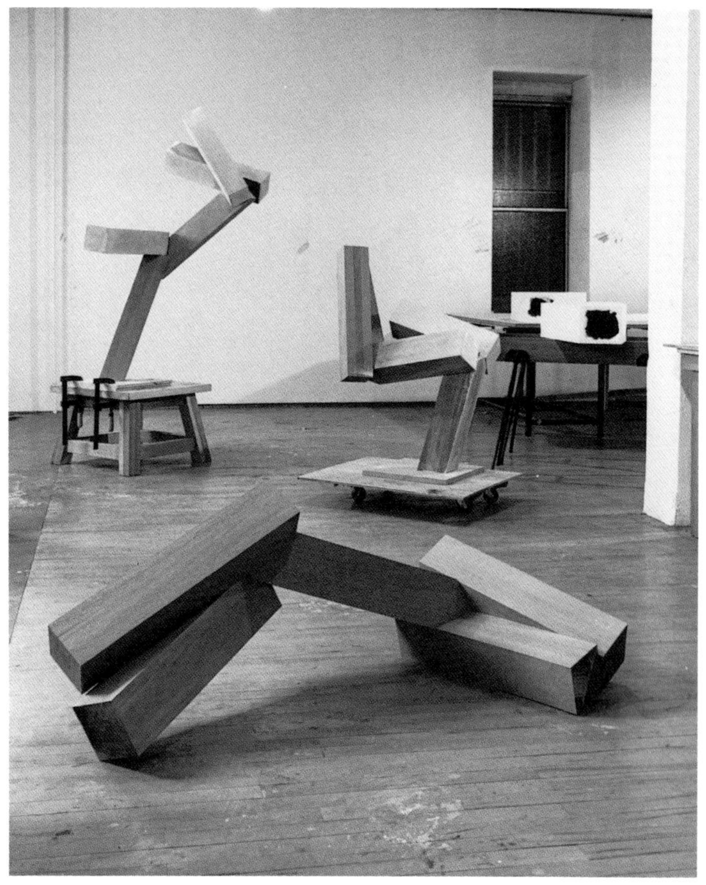

Studio, 1995

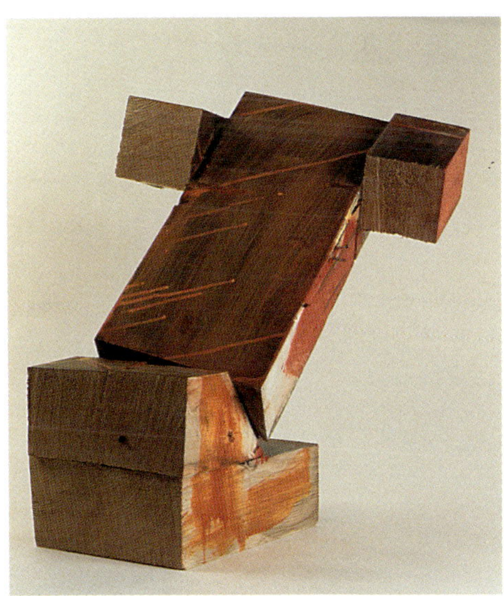

untitled, 1990-91, oil paint on wood, 23 x 21½ x 18"

Although it's not always so clear. Combined with the emotion of the piece, that's something that you can play off of and utilize. Some colors are very natural. Earth colors are so "real world" colors. Other colors are entirely synthetic. So that aspect of color interests me. Color as material, in a way. It's more of a sculptor's approach. There are certain colors you just know: "These things are coded chemical constructs." Maybe they occur on the wing of a kingfisher.

ELLEN:
In a painting, you're always working with a climate of color, bound within the painting. So you're dealing with this incredibly complicated interaction of colors on a plane—its humidity, in a sense—and then everything's altered constantly by any new addition of color. It seems to me that in painting the sculpture there is less of that kind of interaction.

JOEL:
I know what you're talking about, but I think that when painters are painting paintings, they are generally trying—through mark-making and fluidity— to describe a form. Now my form is already described. I always have the form. The form is created, it's there.

The form does not always work. Painting can lead to a reconfiguration of the initial form. Chop off parts, rip the form apart, and reassemble. It is an open process. I can change the facts.

ELLEN:
It's three-dimensional. It's in the round. And therefore, it's also acted on by life in a way that is very different from painting, which is flat to the wall and the light is more constant. So the color that's added to the three-dimensional, in the round pieces, changes radically as the light changes on the pieces as well.

JOEL:
I think that's how you perceive it. When I'm painting it, I do walk around the piece. But how the sculpture unfolds with shadow and light source—that's outside of my control. What I'm after is a synthesis of the color and the form, to describe the intention of the piece. Or sometimes to locate the intention of the piece. I might make a piece that

engages me. But at one point I might lose track of it. I still have the form, but what does it mean? And there can be a rediscovery, via the paint. It depends how powerful the form is, what originally interested me in the piece.

ELLEN:
Do you now—as opposed to previously—make wooden pieces specifically *to* paint?

JOEL:
Yes—but I always have. I've never been interested in the wood aspect. I've gone to great efforts to find wood that wasn't grainy, wood that doesn't look like furniture, wood that doesn't have reference to utilitarian objects. Most of those wood pieces I've painted. I've very rarely left them alone.

But what *has* changed, is that when I began to work with wood, the forms were quite simple. And I could find standardized chunks of wood that read "lumberyard." They were four by fours, two by fours, and the wood had been cut by somebody else. So it was, more or less, a case of finding lumber that was suitable, or having lumber around that was suitable for my use at that time. And I think, as the forms became more complicated and larger, as I got more involved, I had to make the lumber. And in the *making*, there is a considerable amount of craft that goes on. And I think craft can become a focus and undermine the idea.

ELLEN:
When you say you make the lumber, in other words, you're not using the standard four by four. You decide to use eight by eight. That means you have to join and glue pieces together?

JOEL:
Right. You can't just take big chunks of green lumber from a sawmill and use them, because they just crack to pieces. I have to make the timbers in my studio from smaller pieces. So now there's a more elaborate process in creating the form, and paint's been very *useful* as a mask.

I'm somebody who just isn't too keen on wood sculpture. I'm not that interested in the way wood looks. I'm interested in the speed with which you can make a form with wood, and how the wood absorbs—and affects the color of—the paint.

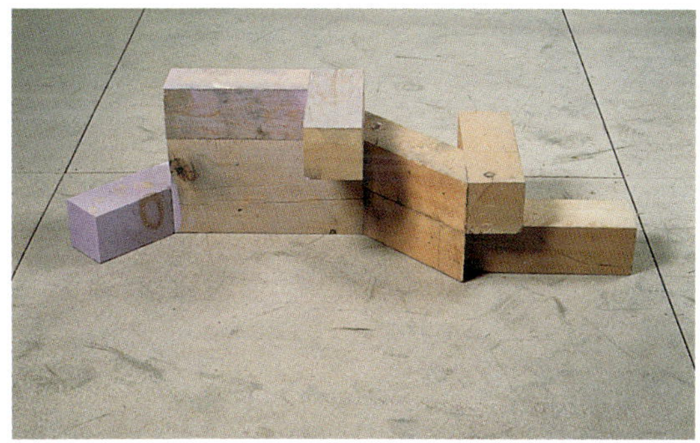

untitled, 1982, oil paint on wood, 12 ³/₈ x 43 ¼ x 13 ¼"

ELLEN:

An earlier figurative piece in which the most minimal use of paint really alters your perception of the conventional monolithic quality of sculpture is the 1982 piece that Doug Cramer owns.

JOEL:

It's a good example: the head's lavender, and the head kind of disappears, and the head becomes much more thoughtful juxtaposed against the physicality of the unpainted wood of the rest of the piece. Now, with the recent work, the big one that's painted gray (pp. 44-45), I had the structure here. It's a relatively old structure. And I looked at it and began to put layers of thin paint on it, according to the form. Just to reinforce its lightness and its airiness. And that's enough.

ELLEN:

So the gray paint, which is very close in value to the color of the unpainted wood, is concentrated at the most complex joint.

JOEL:

Yes. Now the paint on that *other* piece, the one with cylinders, that I've used pastel on (p. 25). I think it radically transforms the separate elements. It really makes a difference. It finishes them. It unifies them. It animates them. It takes them away from the realm of just wood. That kind of utilization of paint and color is exactly what is interesting to me, because it has a metaphoric reading.

I still think there are lots of possibilities.

Ellen Phelan is a painter and Professor of the Practice of Studio Arts at Harvard University, and the wife of Joel Shapiro.

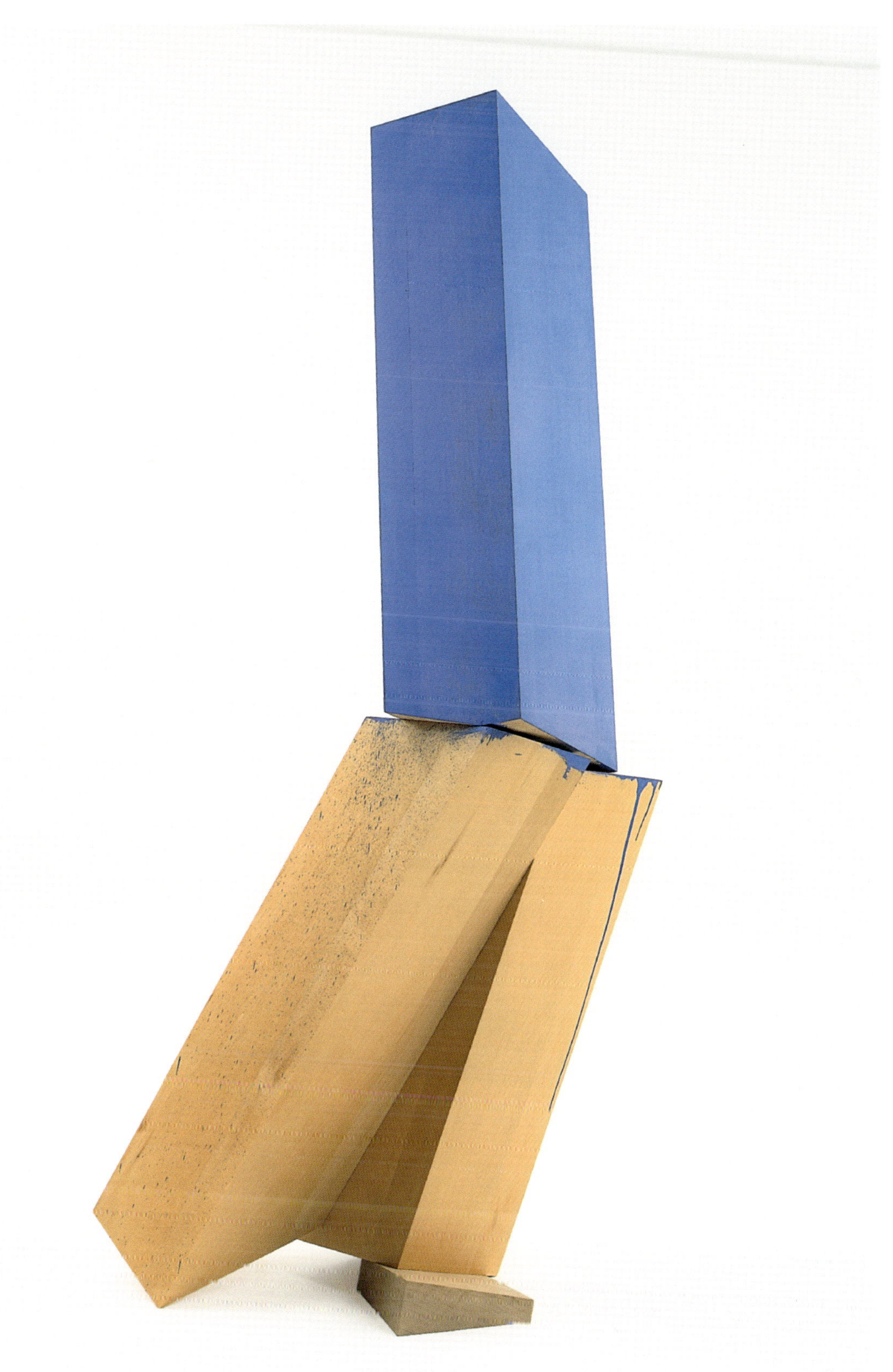

untitled, 1994, oil paint on wood, 47 x 13 x 18 ½″

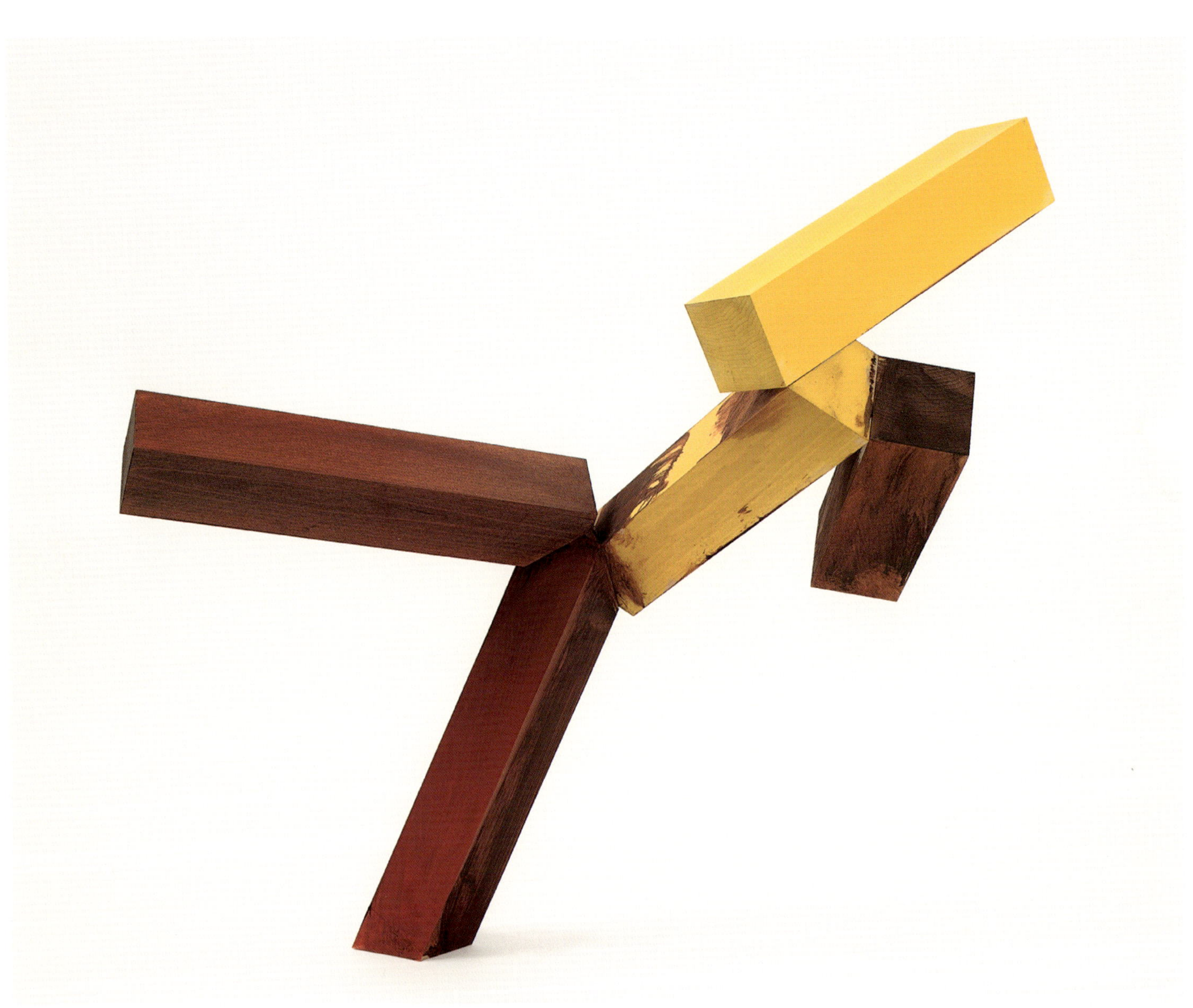

untitled, 1994, oil paint on wood, 29 ½ x 32 x 22", view 1

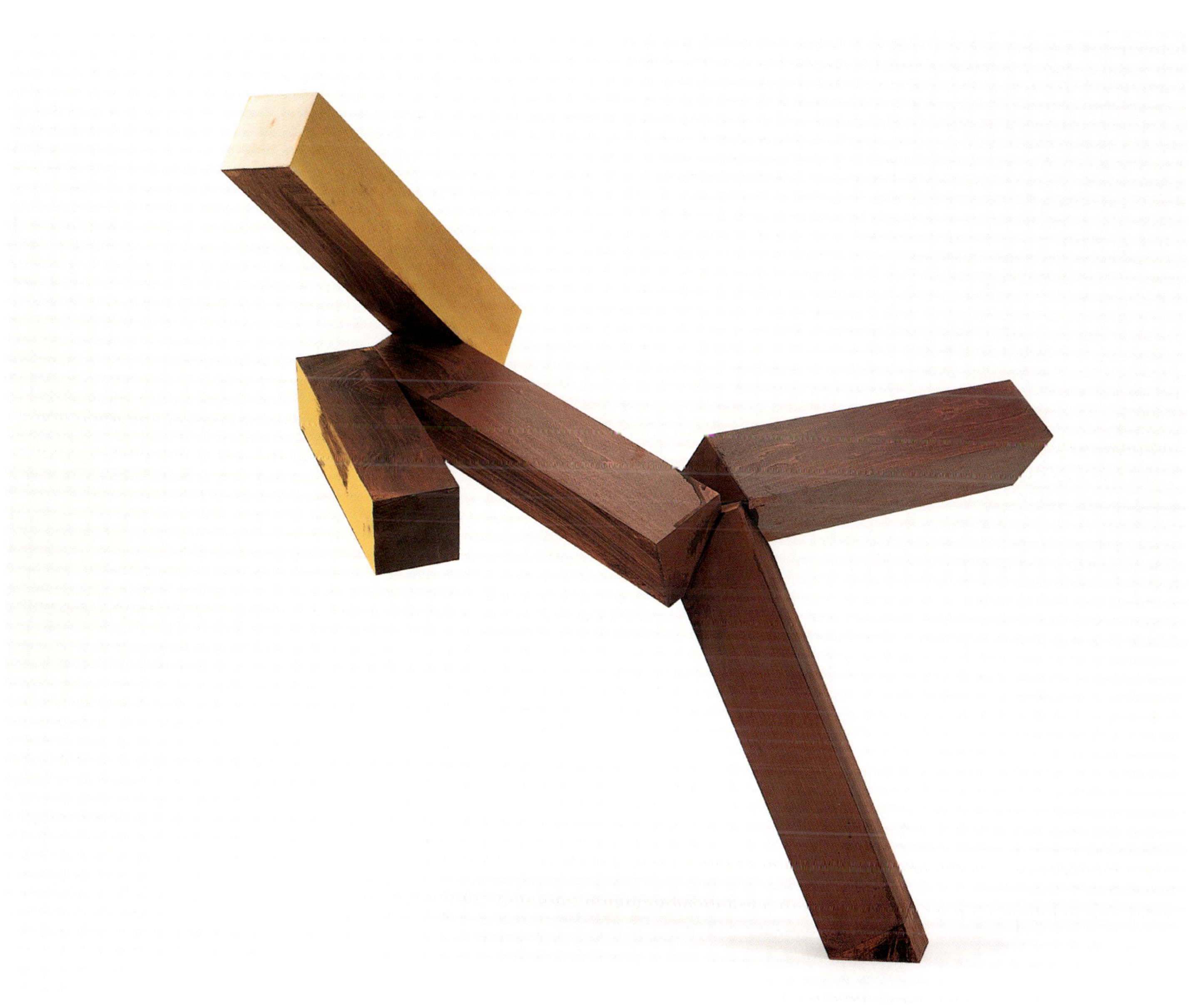

untitled, 1994, oil paint on wood, 29 ½ x 32 x 22″, view 2

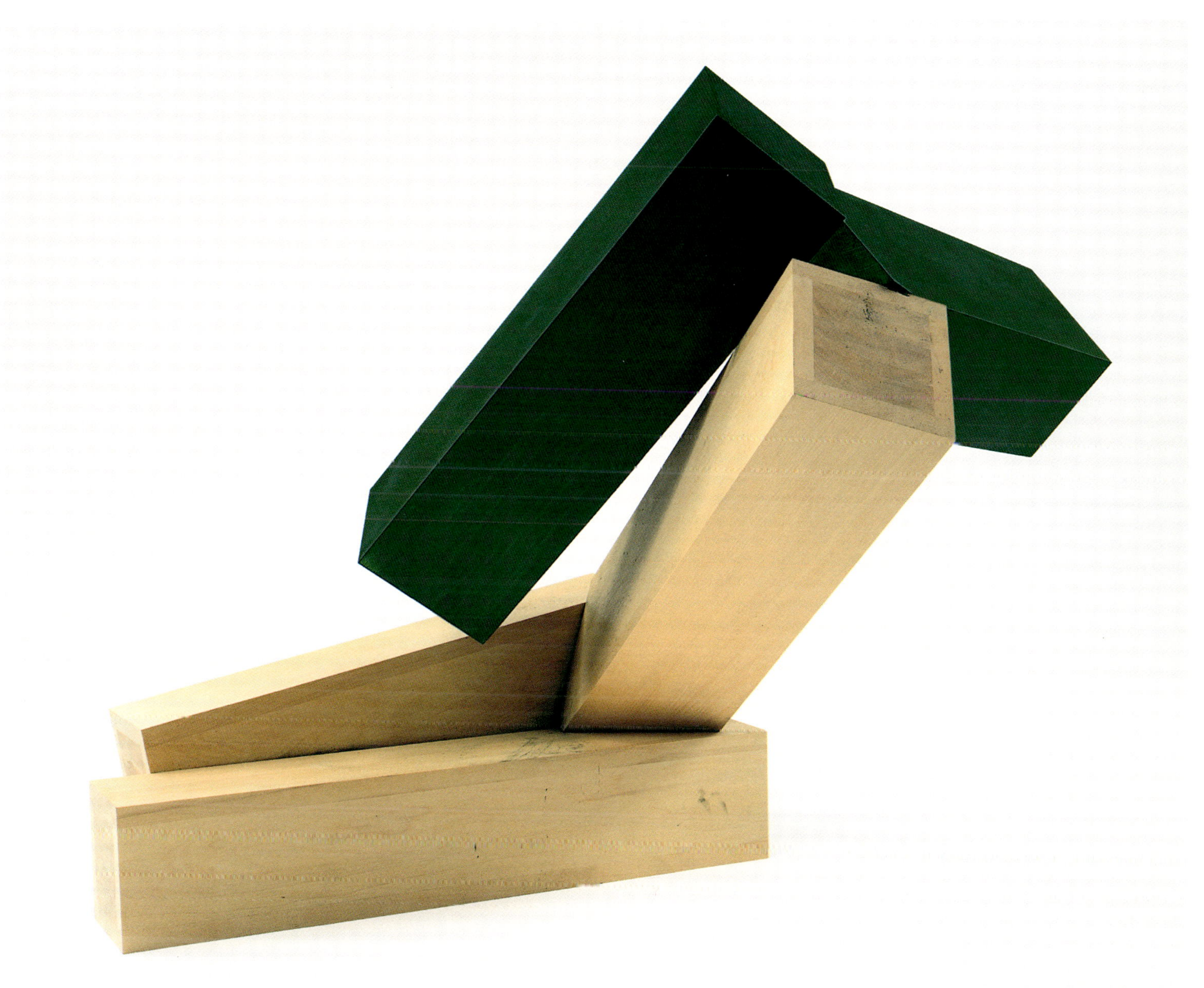

untitled, 1990-94, oil paint on wood, 31 x 45 x 28"

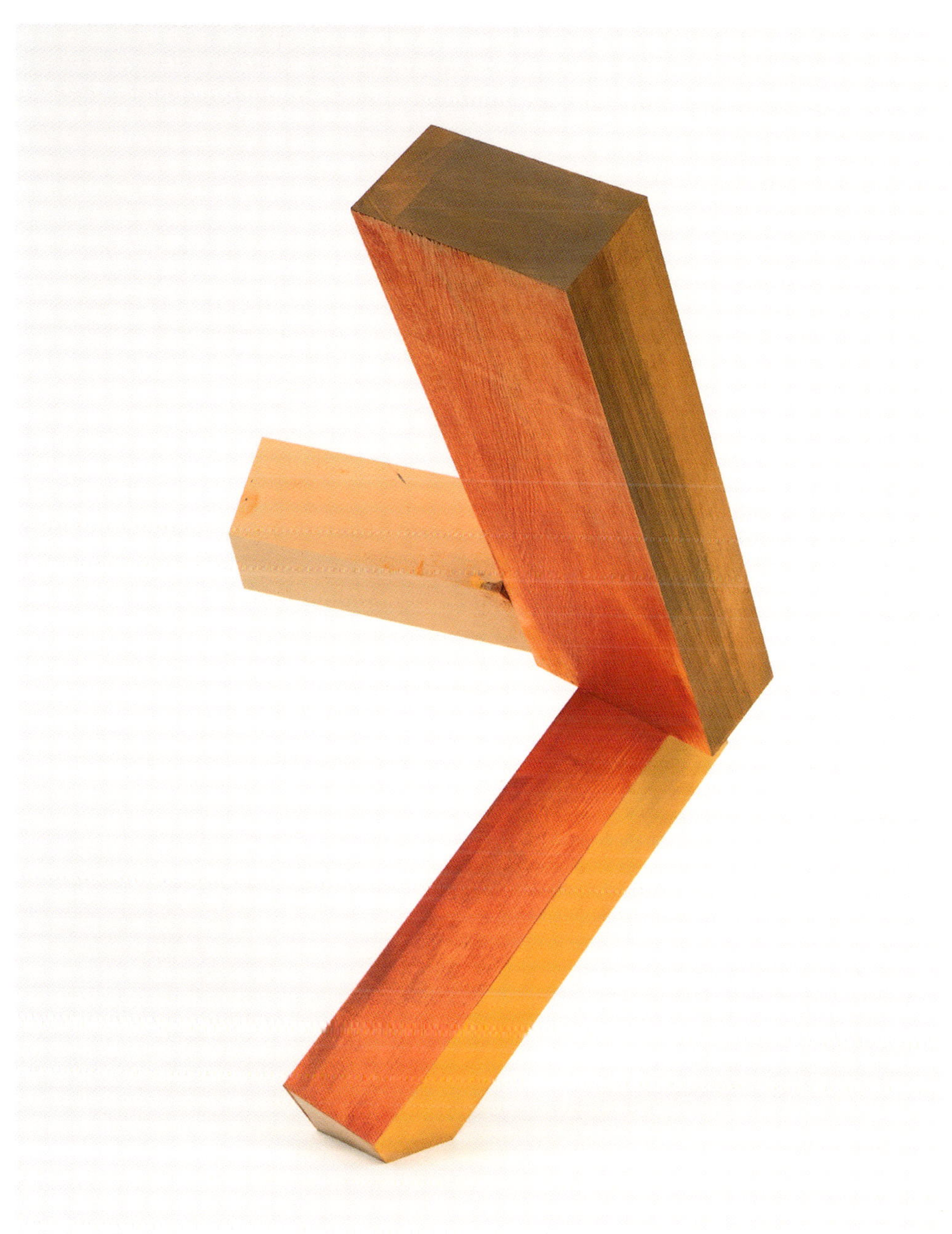

untitled, 1993, oil paint on wood, 25 3/4 x 21 x 20"

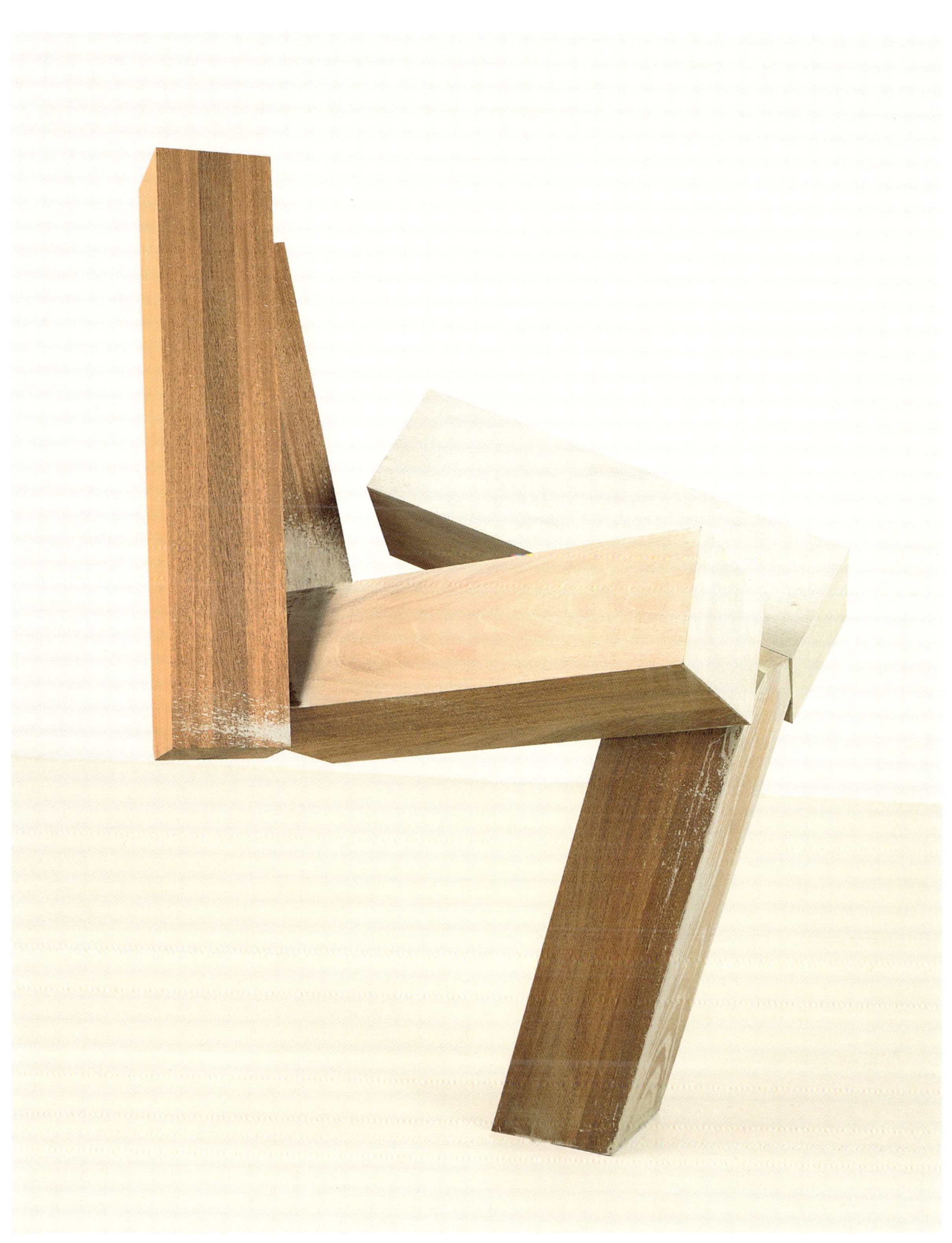

untitled, 1994-95, oil paint on wood, 46 x 36 x 21"

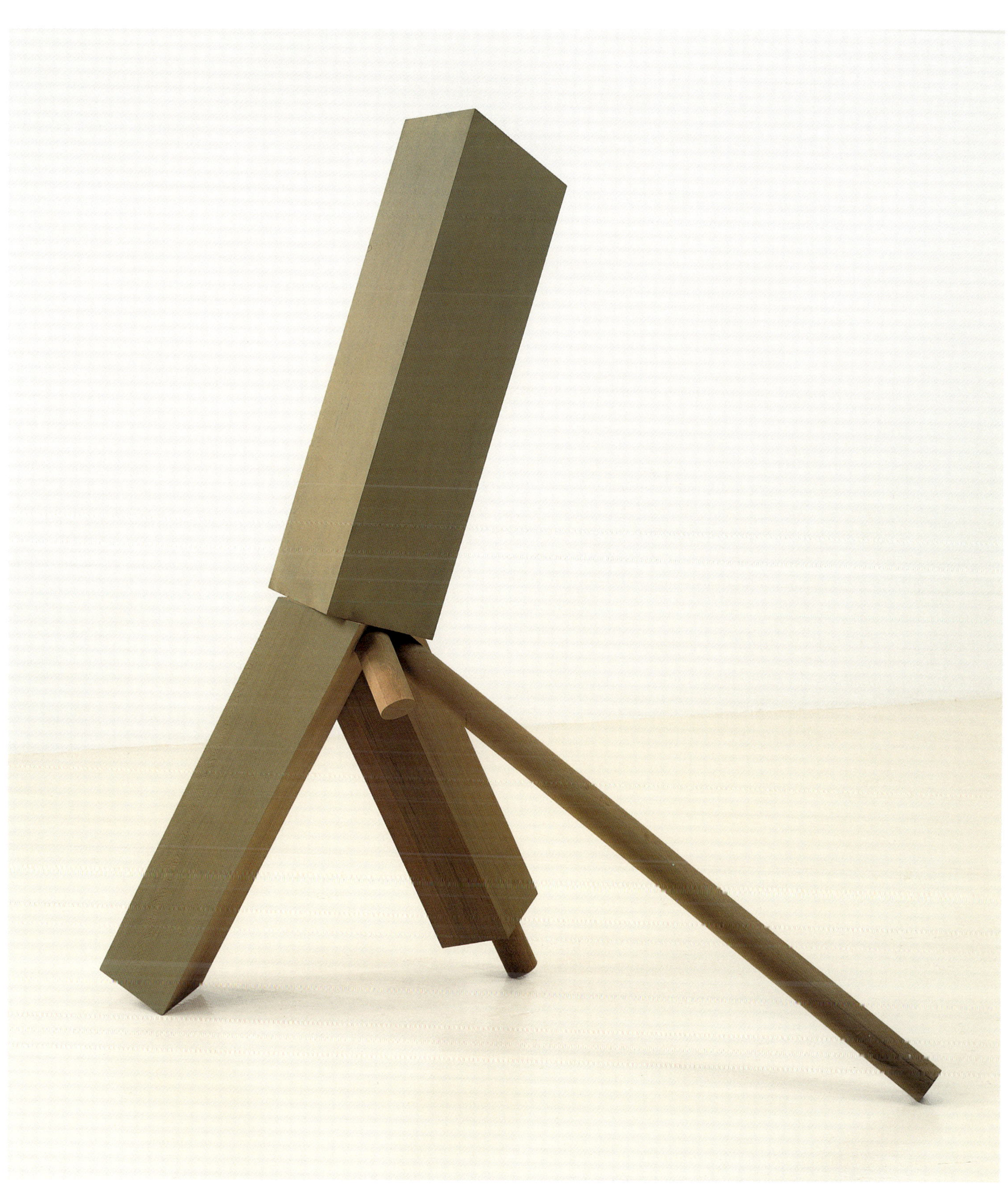

untitled, 1993, oil paint and pastel on wood, 53 x 54 x 22"

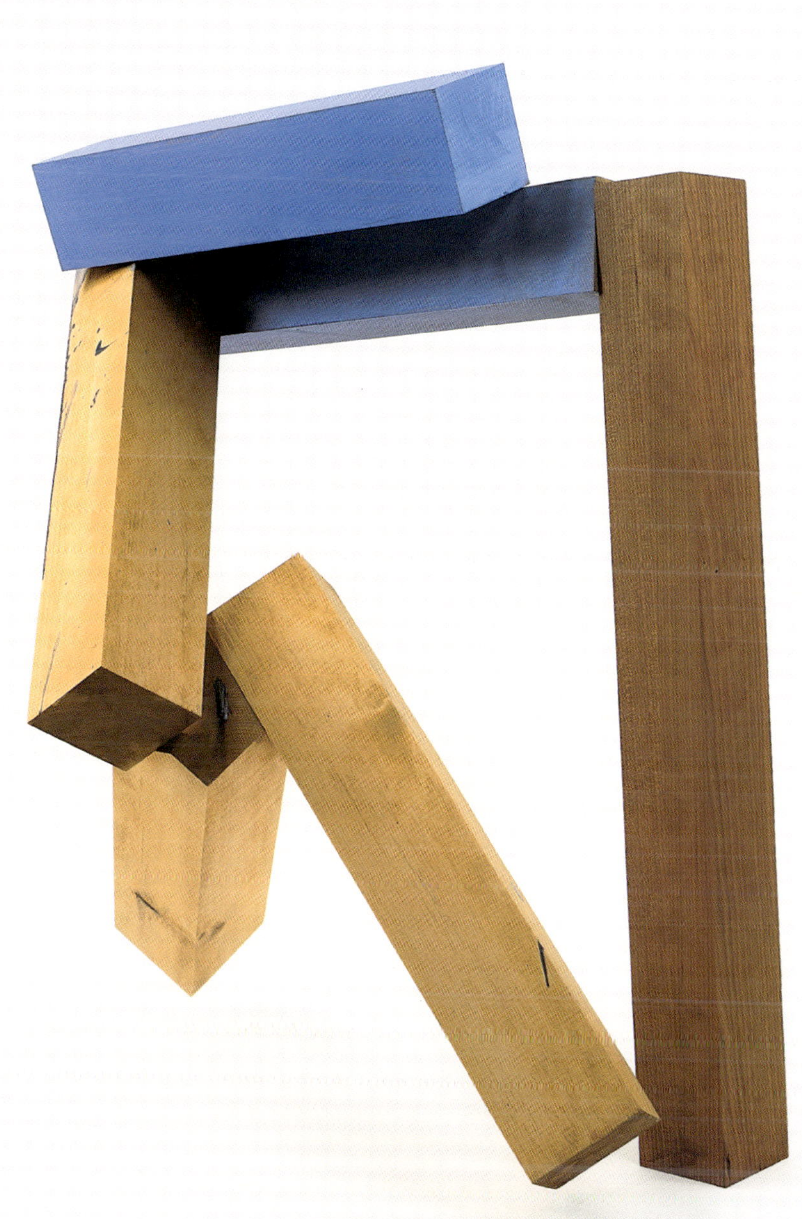

untitled, 1994, oil paint on wood, 33 x 30 x 18 ″

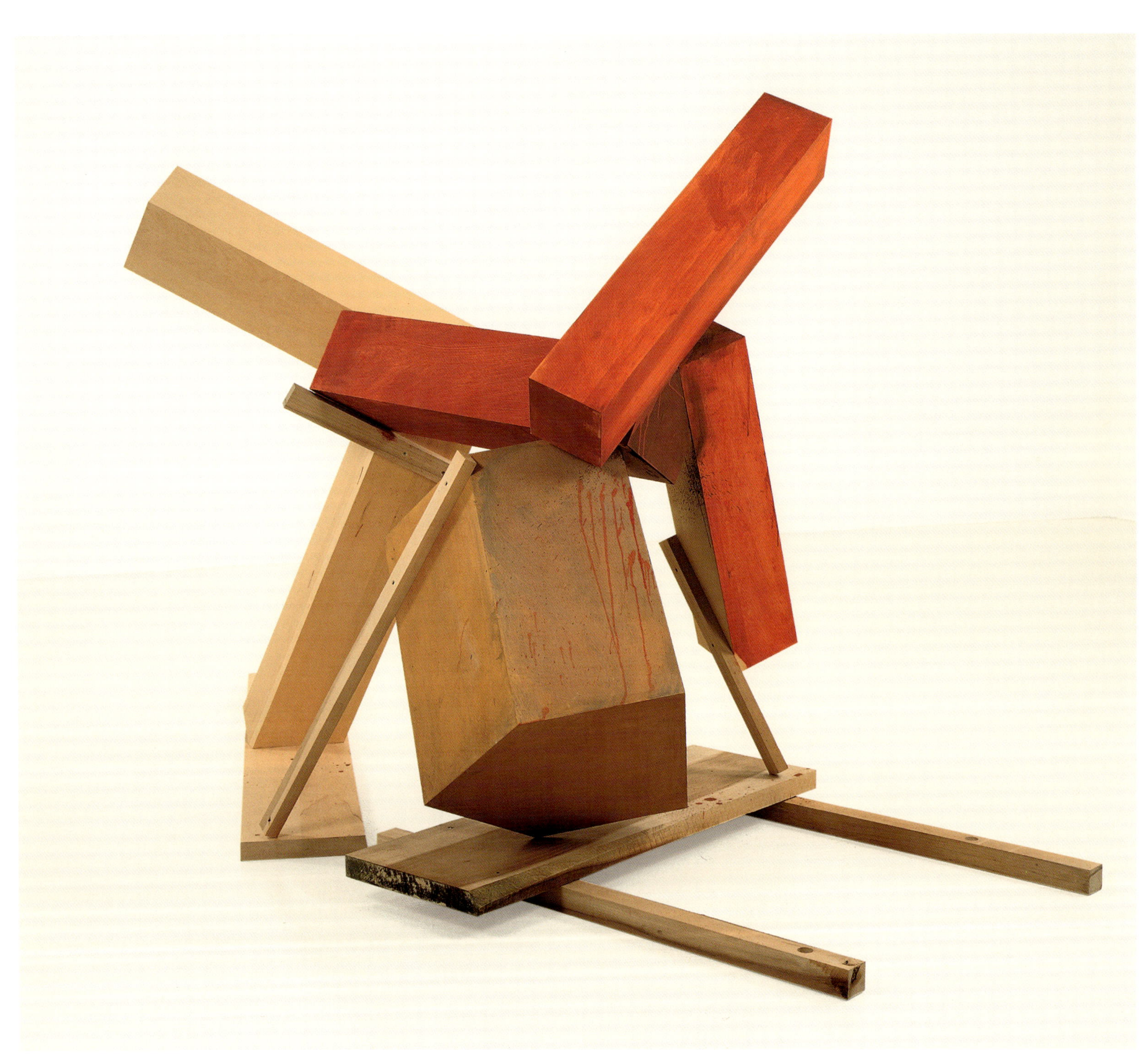

untitled, 1993-94, oil paint on wood, 65 x 111 x 52", view 1

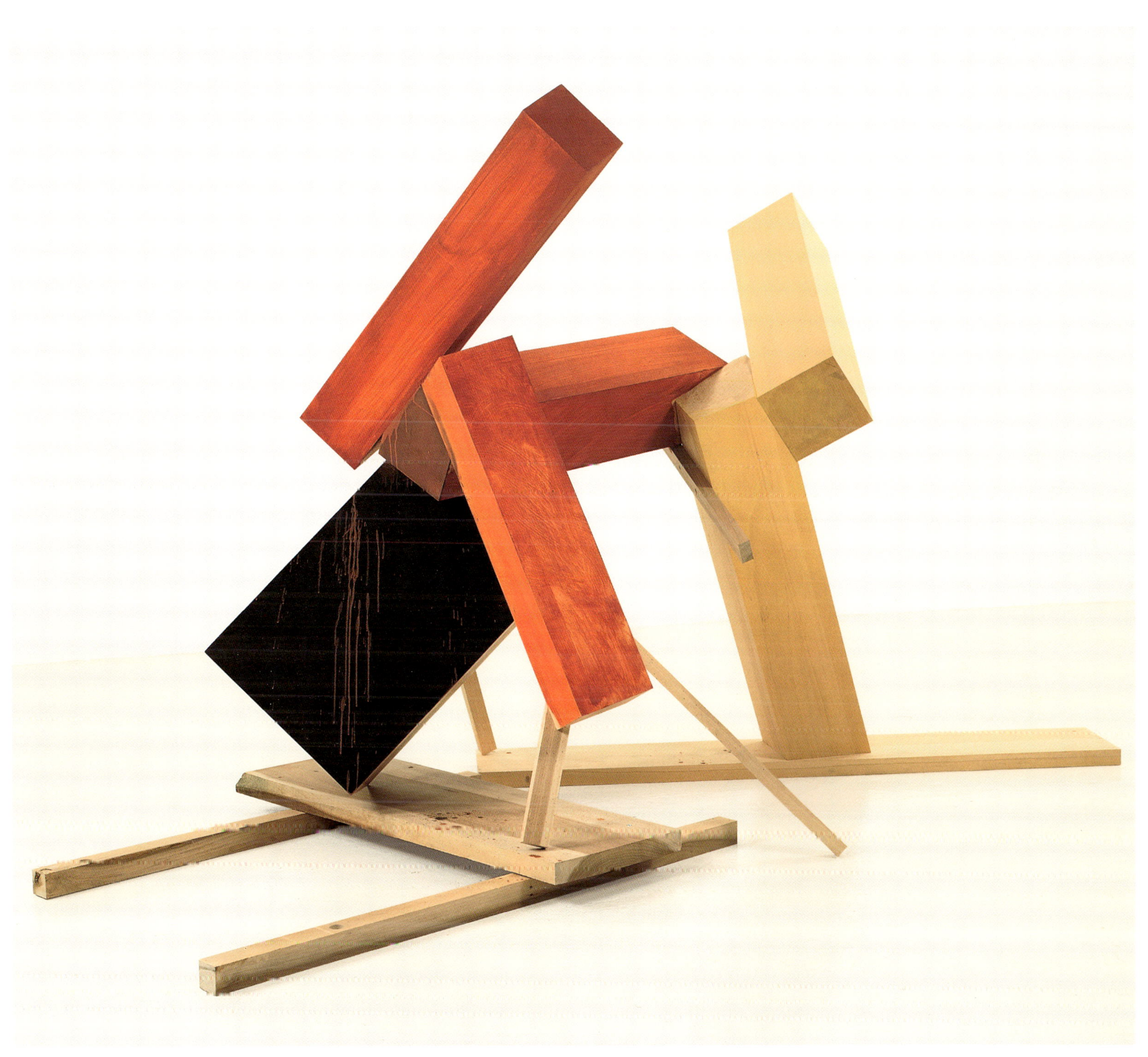

untitled, 1993-94, oil paint on wood, 65 x 111 x 52", view 2

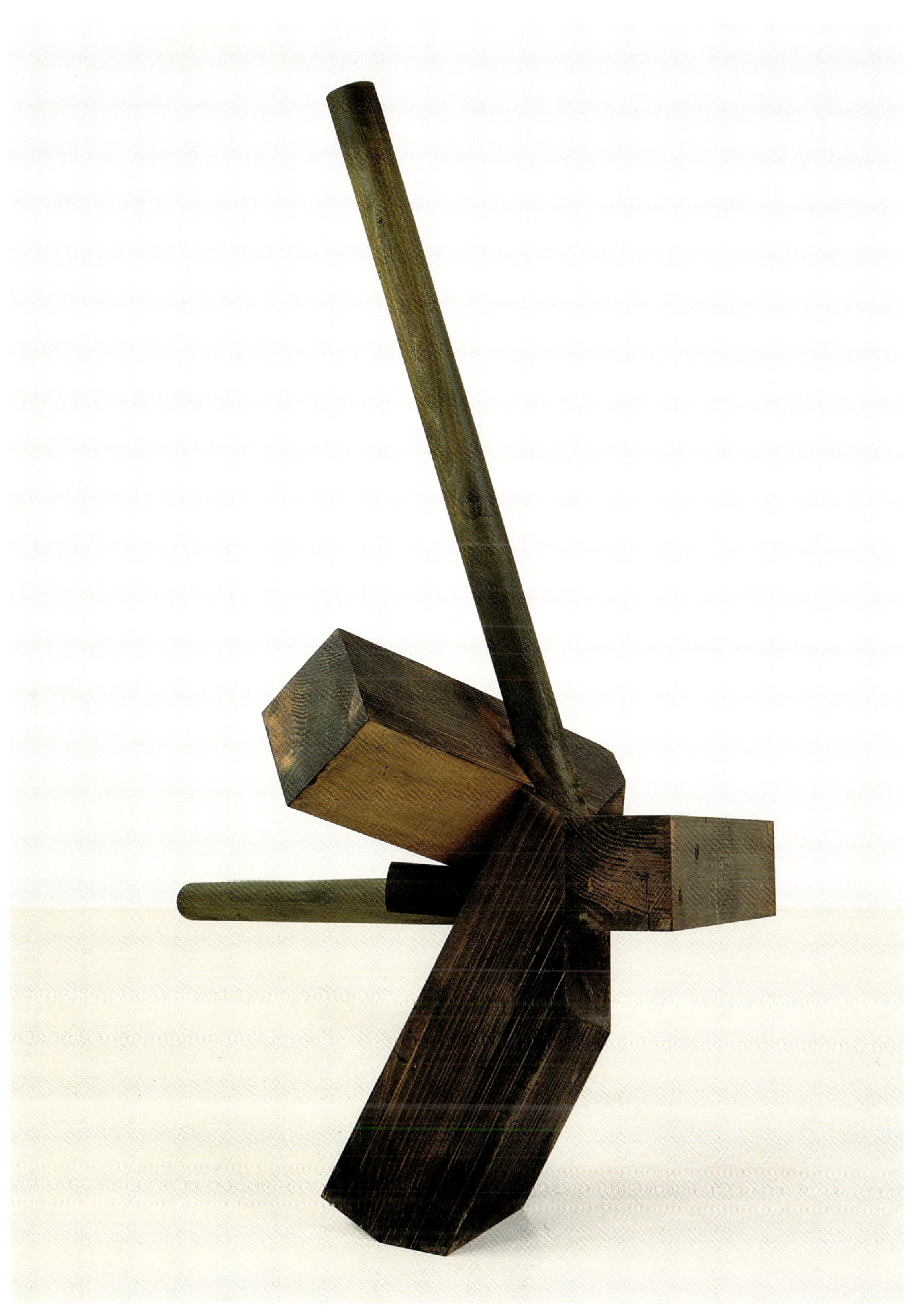

untitled, 1992-95, oil paint on wood, 55 1/2 x 53 x 34"

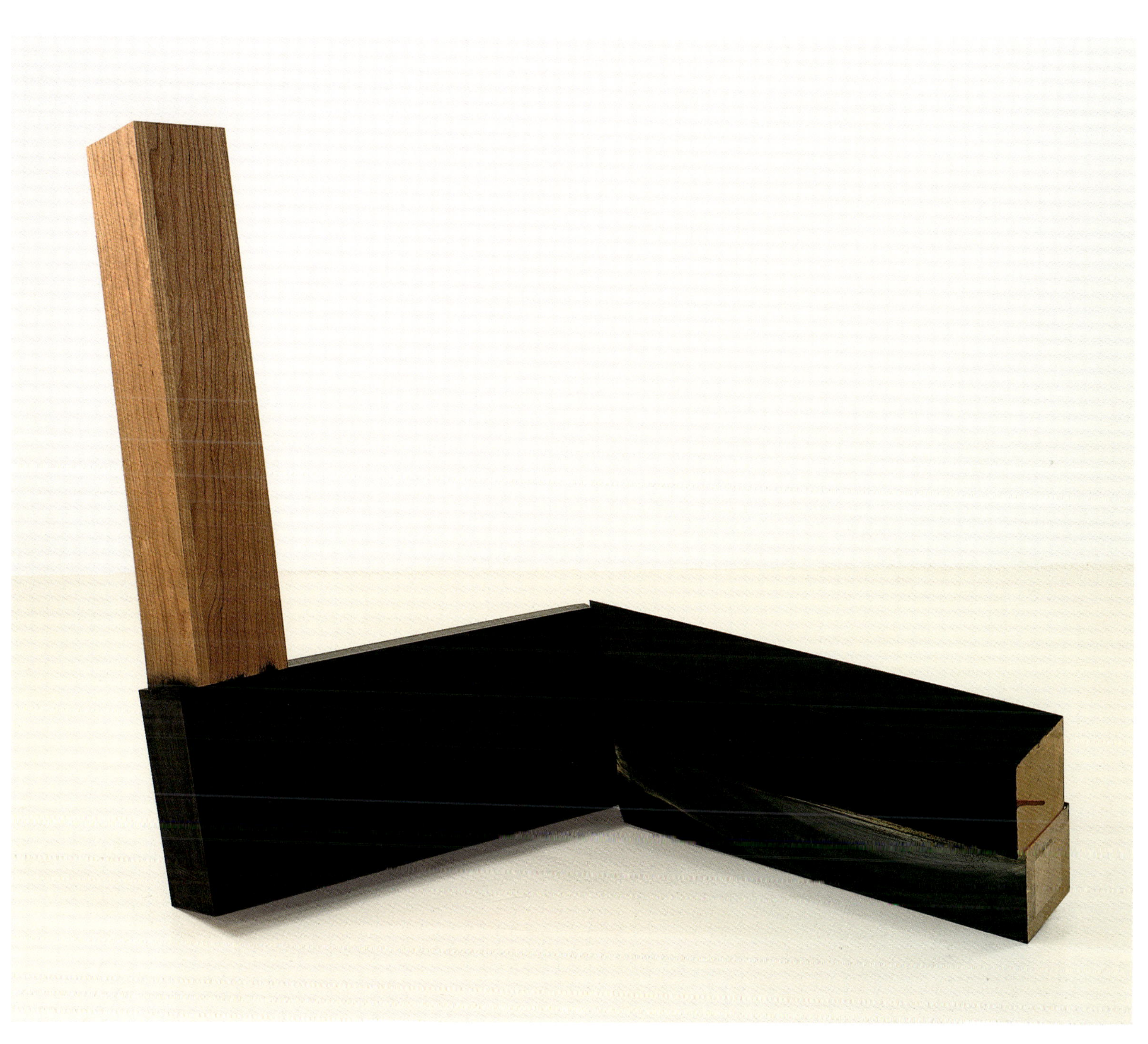

untitled, 1994-95, oil paint on wood, 46 x 60 x 32"

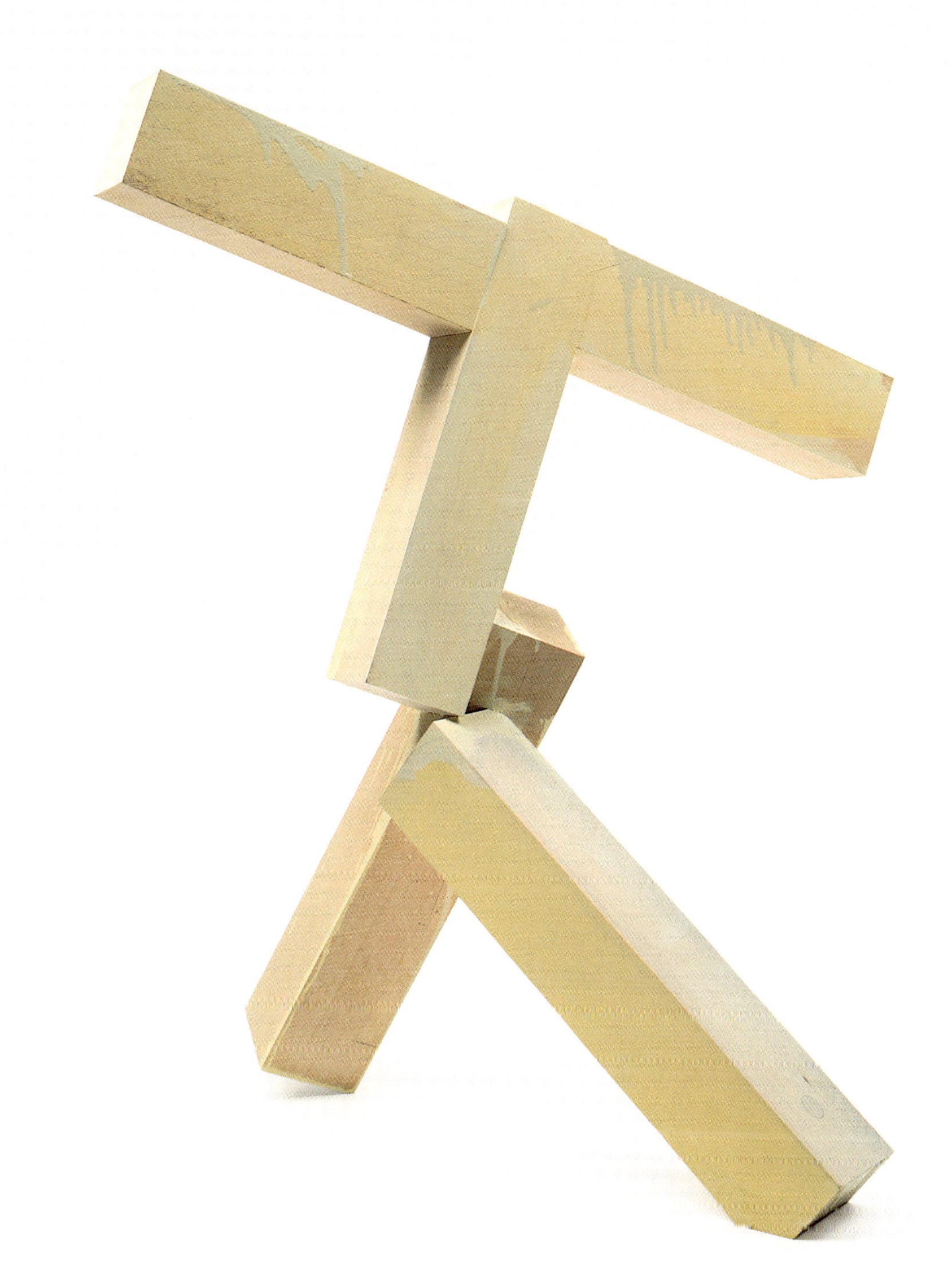

untitled, 1994, oil paint on wood, 26 x 16 x 21"

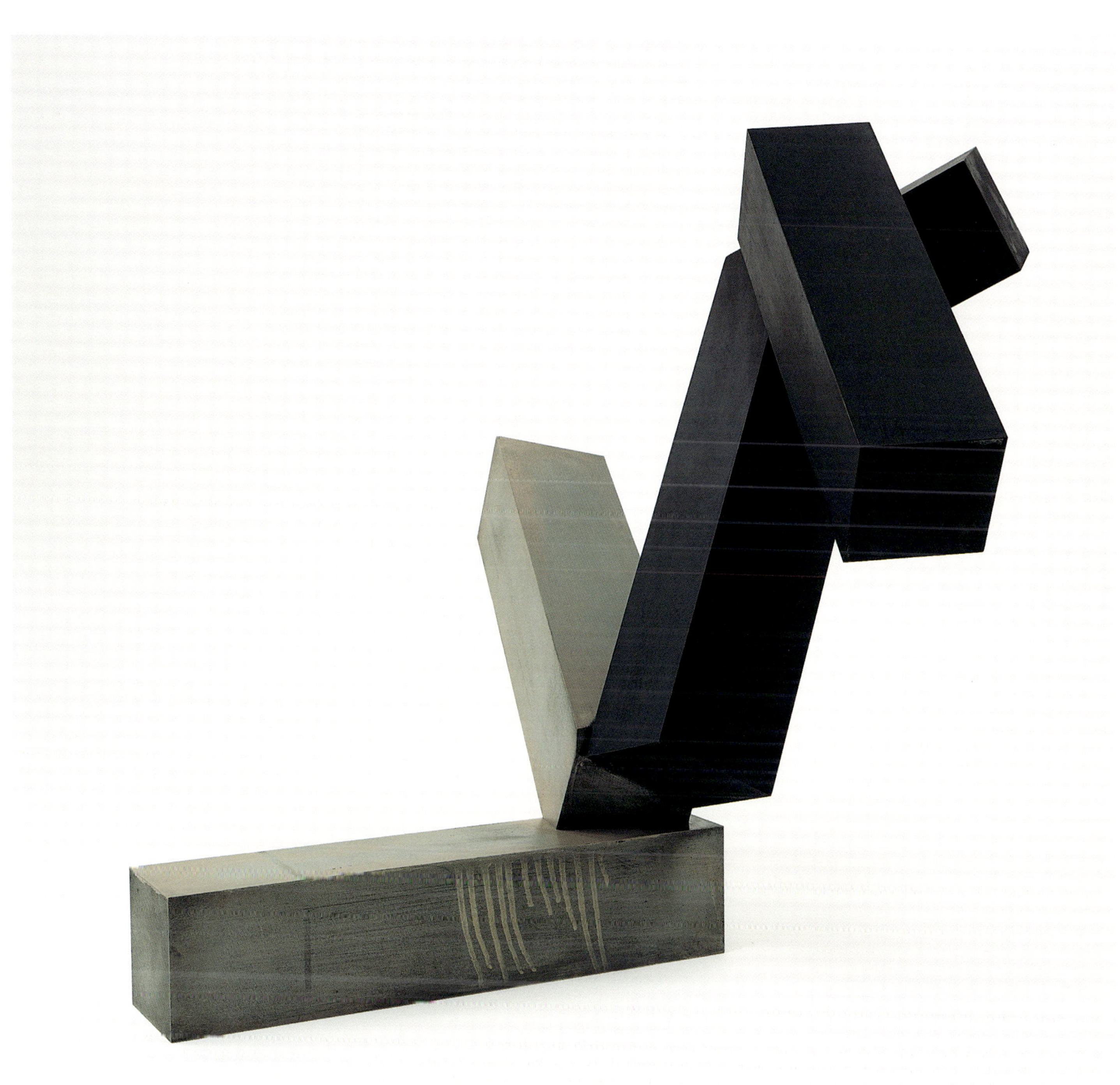

untitled, 1994-95, oil paint on wood, 29 x 36 x 34"

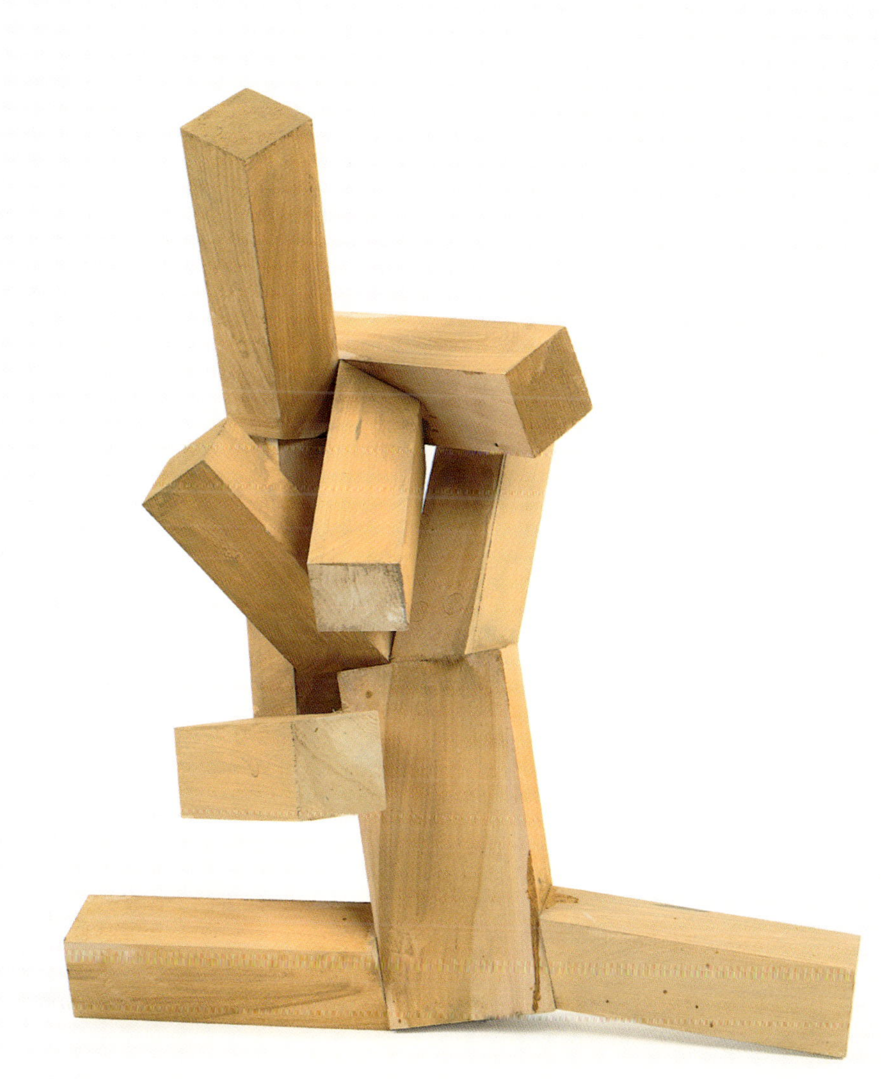

untitled, 1993-94, oil paint on wood, 19 x 17 x 15″

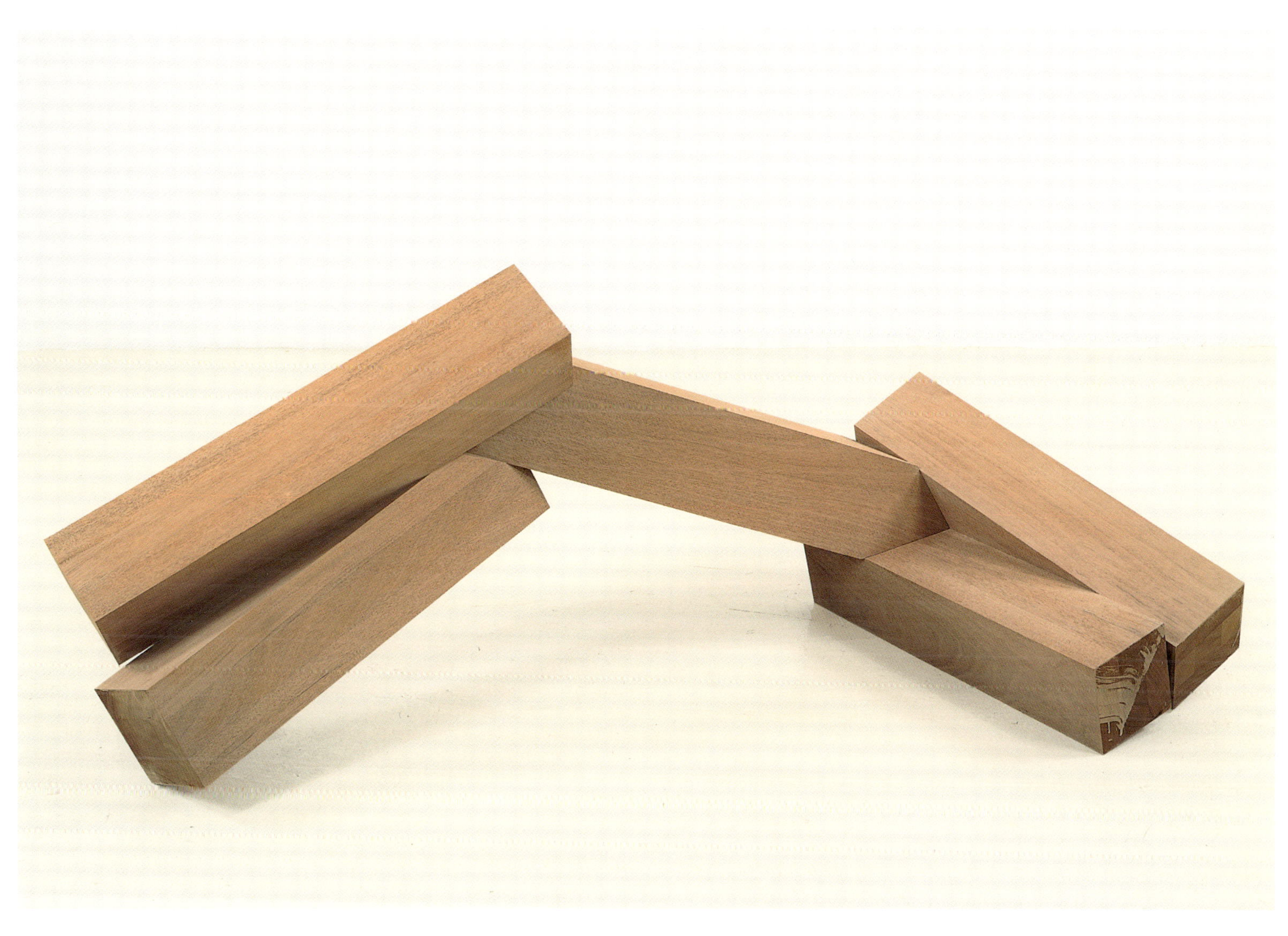

untitled, 1995, oil paint on wood, 23 x 61 x 32"

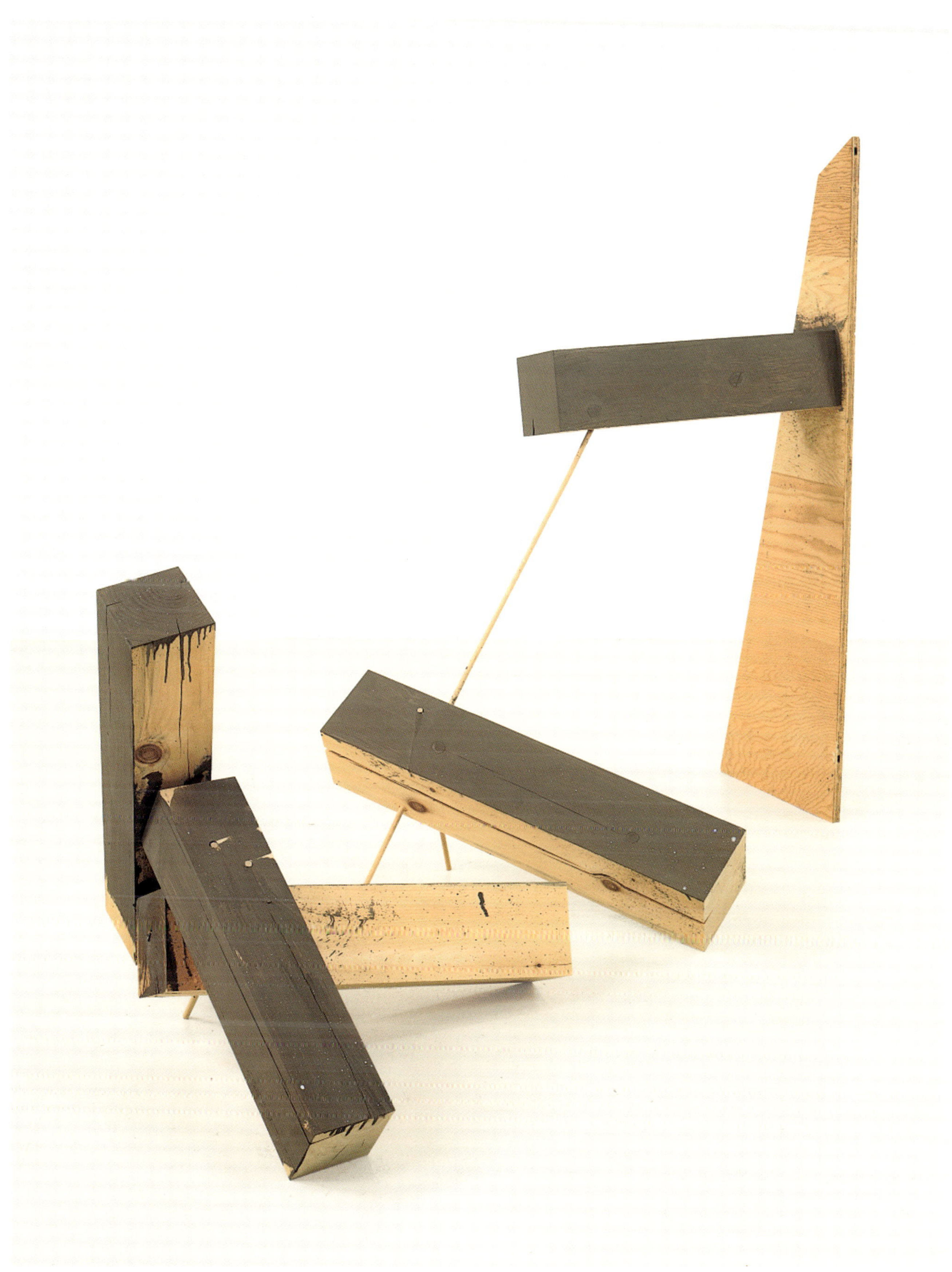

untitled, 1993, oil paint on wood, 47 ½ x 76 x 46"

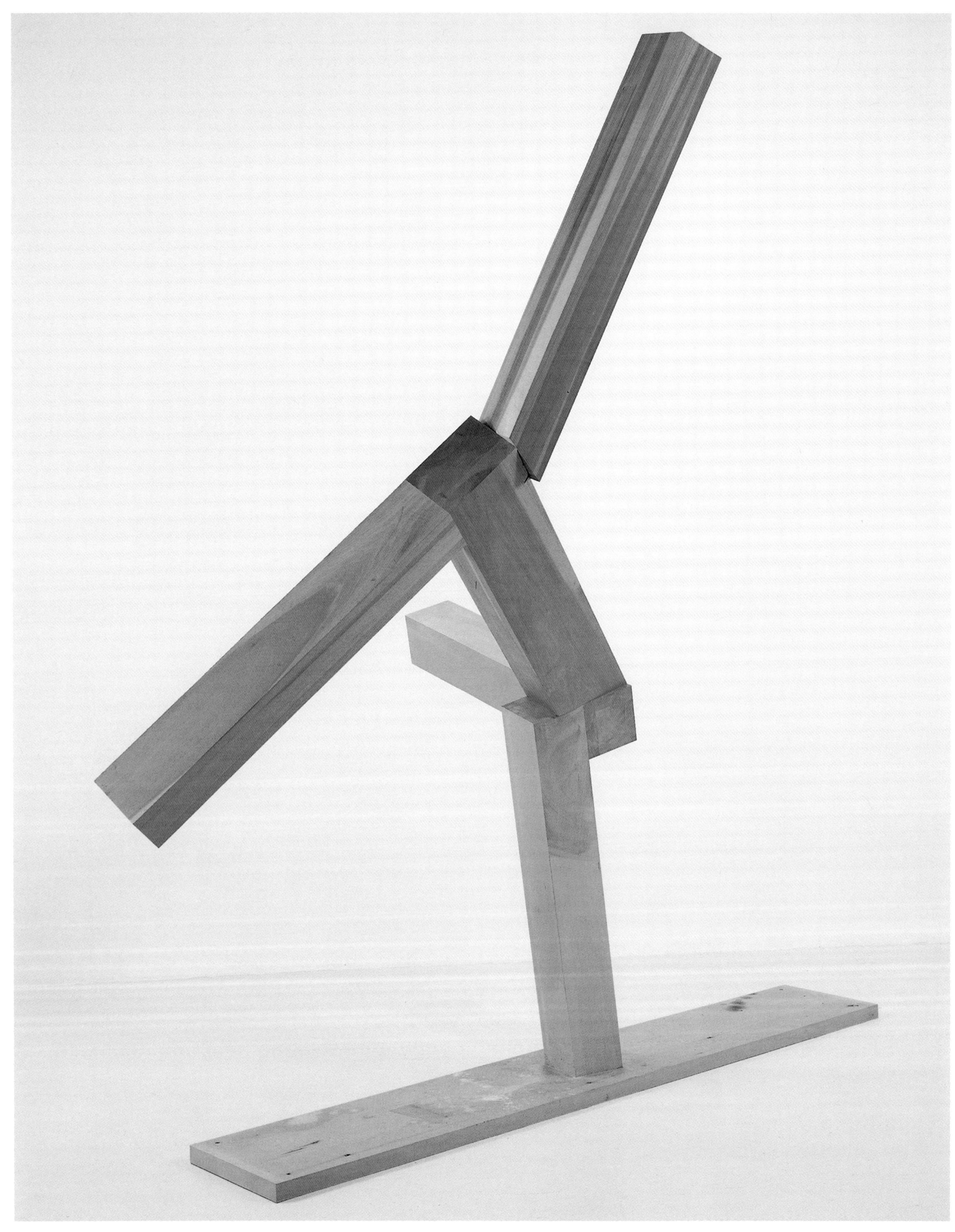

untitled, 1990-94, oil paint on wood, 110 x 120 x 77", view 1

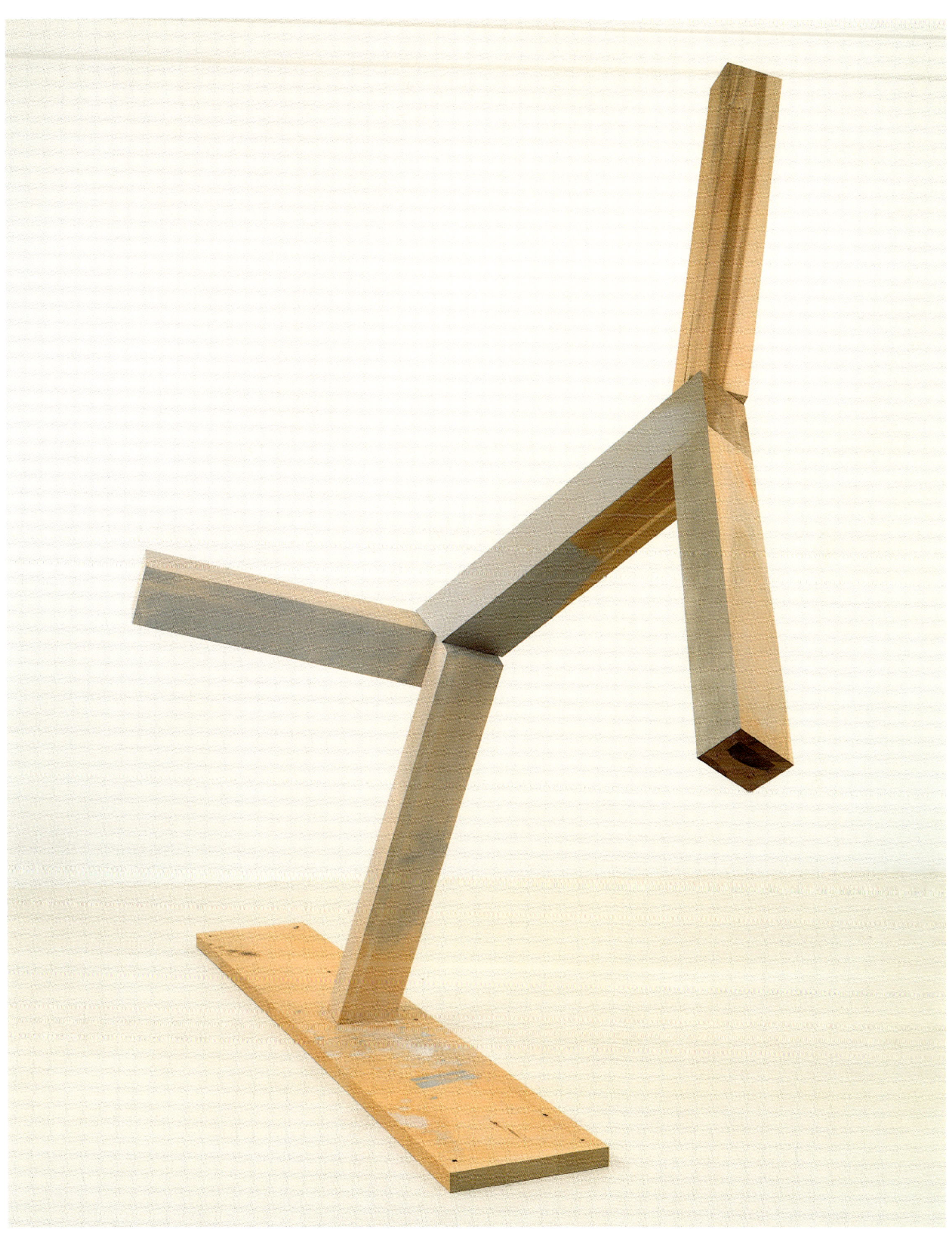

untitled, 1990-94, oil paint on wood, 110 x 120 x 77", view 2   45

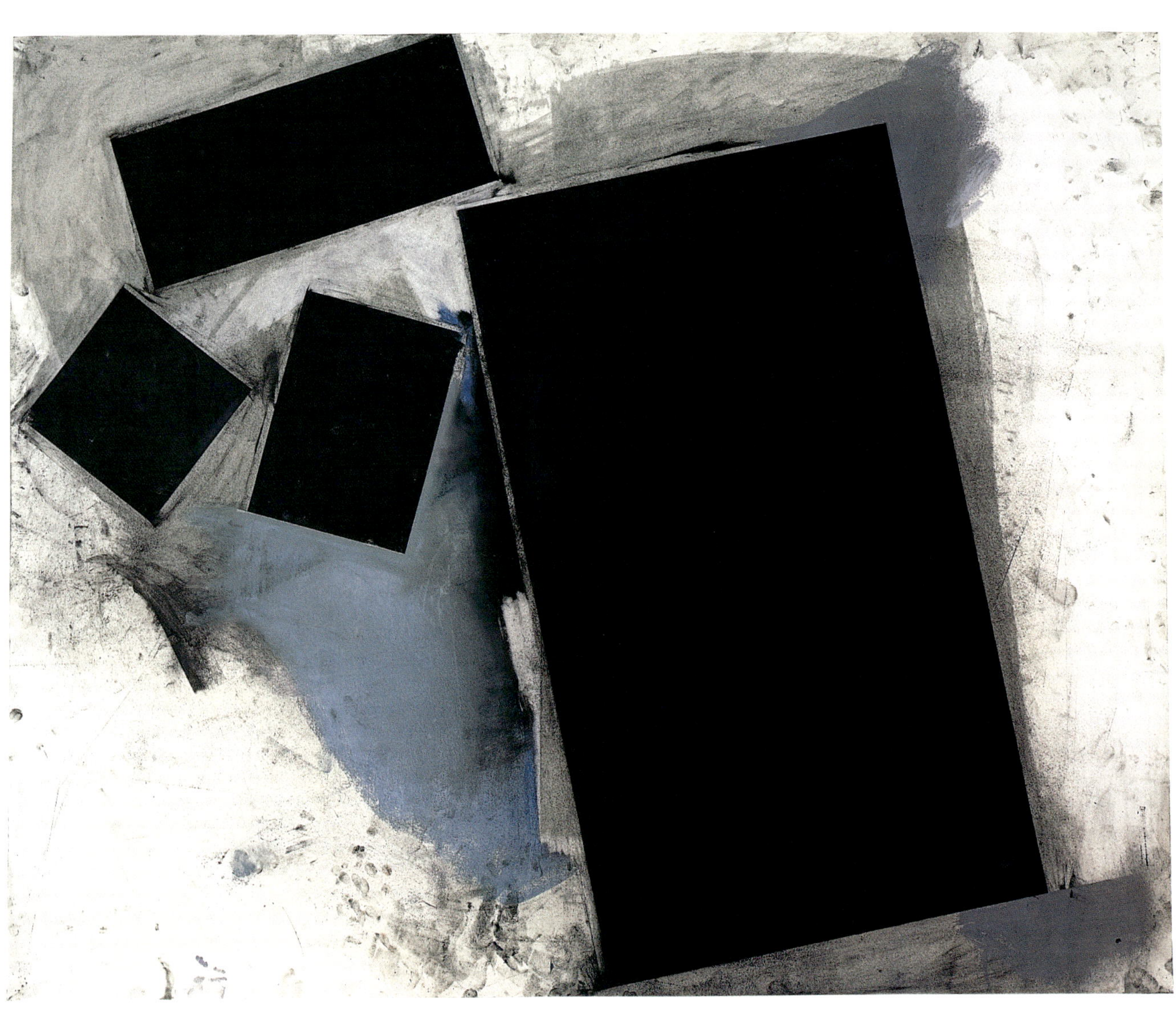

untitled, 1994-95, chalk, charcoal and pastel on paper, 47 x 58"

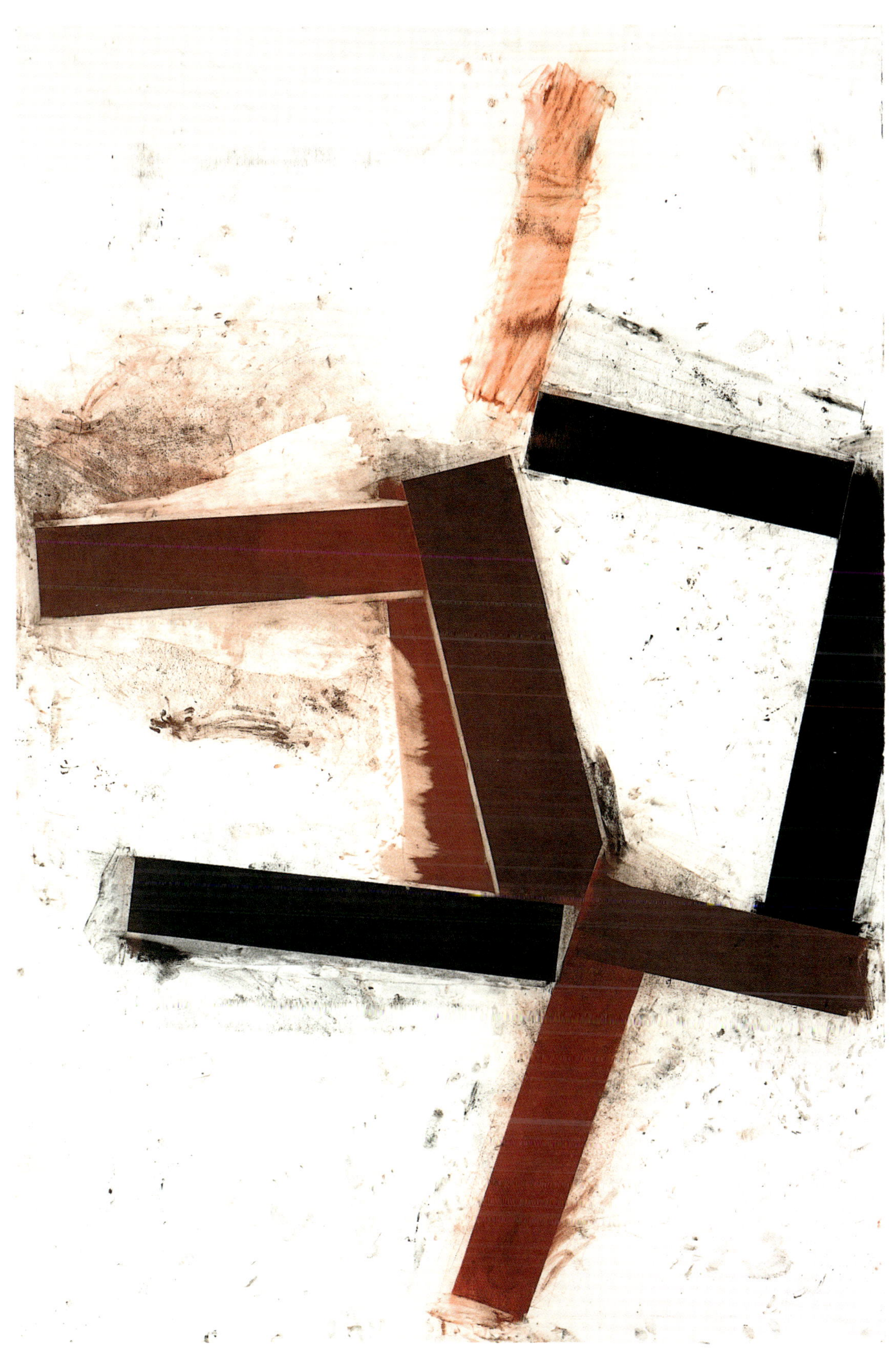

untitled, 1994, chalk, charcoal and pastel on paper, 89 x 60¼"

untitled, 1995, chalk and pastel on paper, 58 x 47"

untitled, 1994, chalk, charcoal and pastel on paper, 58 x 47"

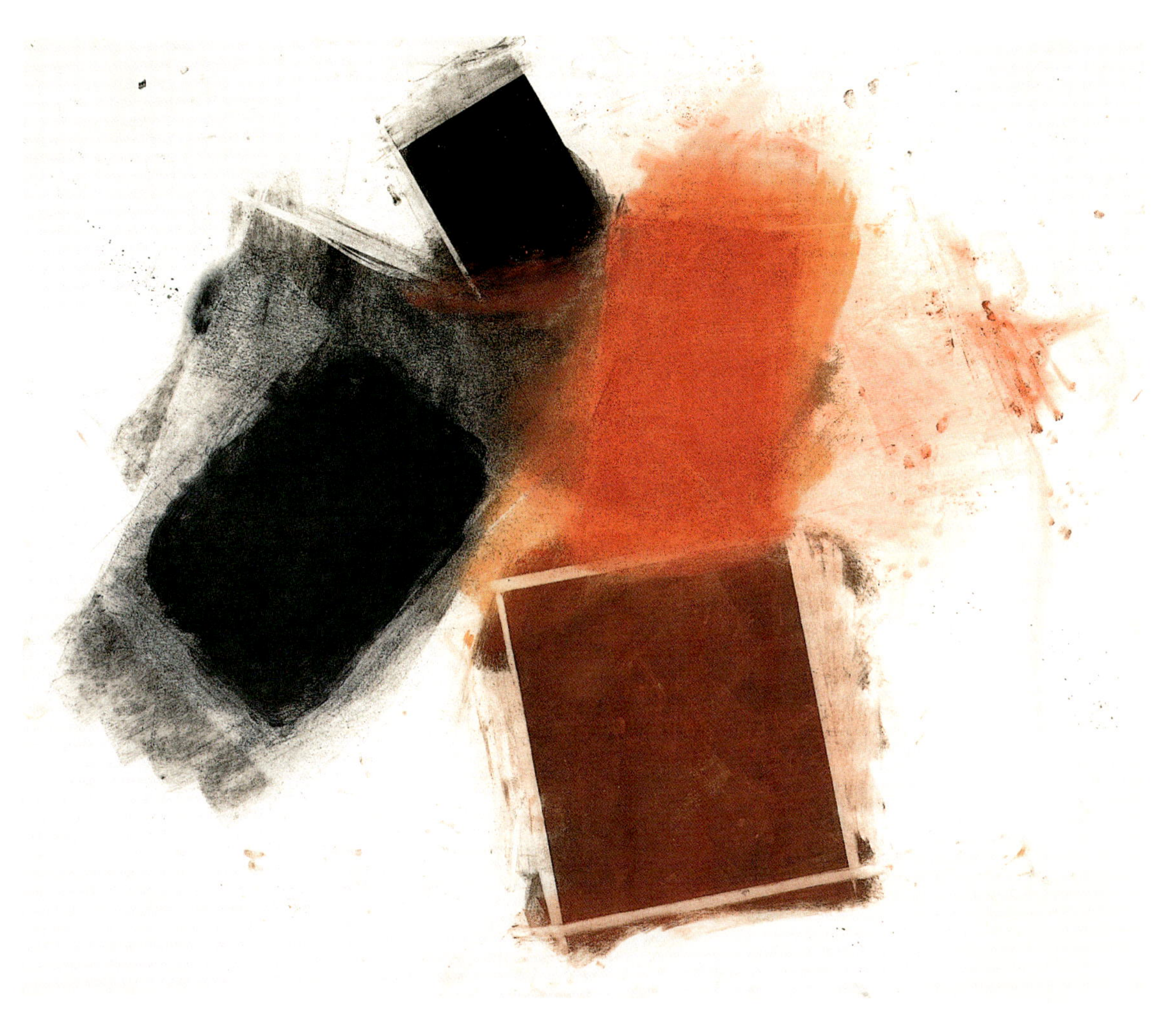

untitled, 1994-95, chalk, charcoal and pastel on paper, 38 x 46"

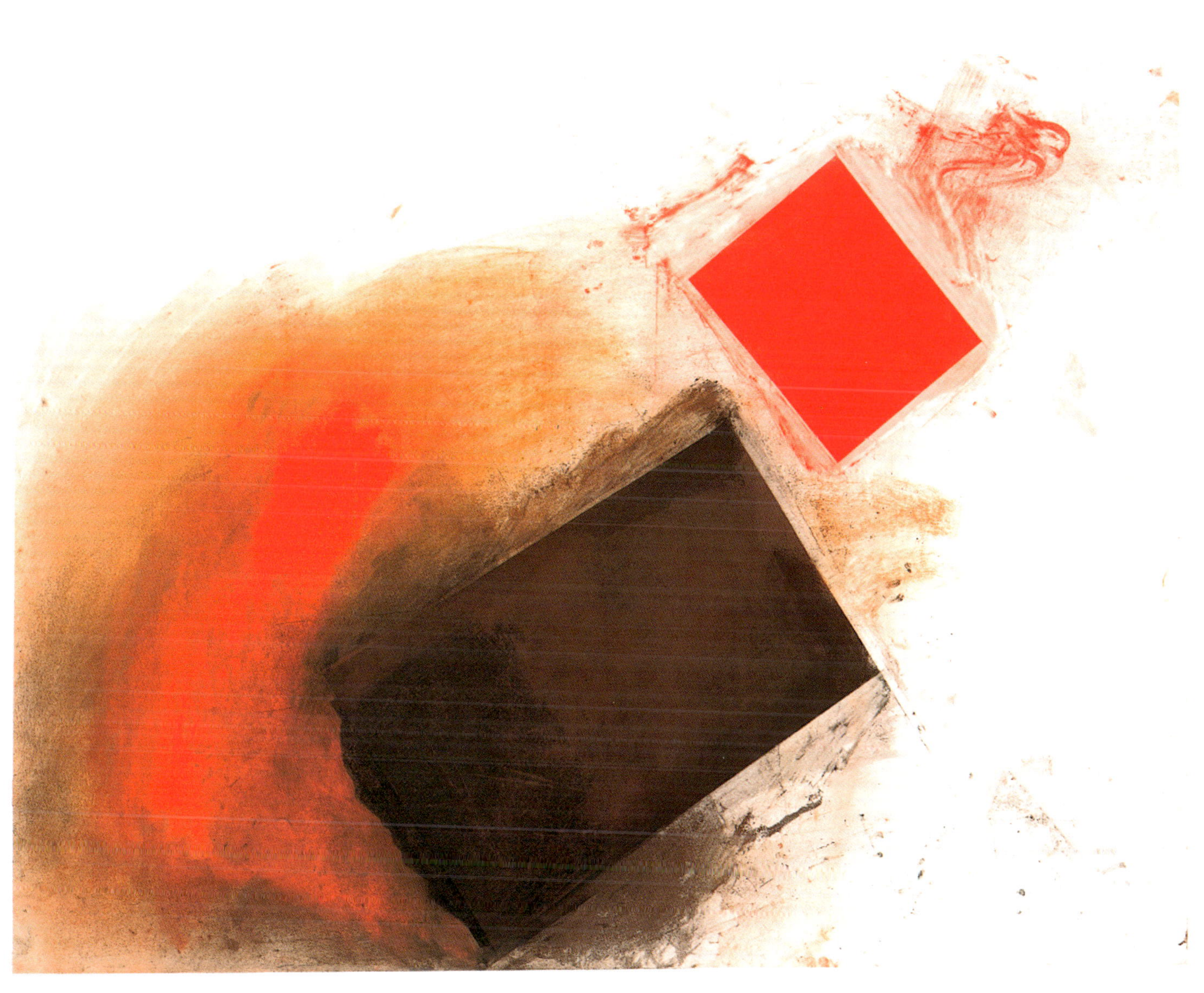

untitled, 1995, chalk, charcoal and pastel on paper, 44 ½ x 57 ⅞"

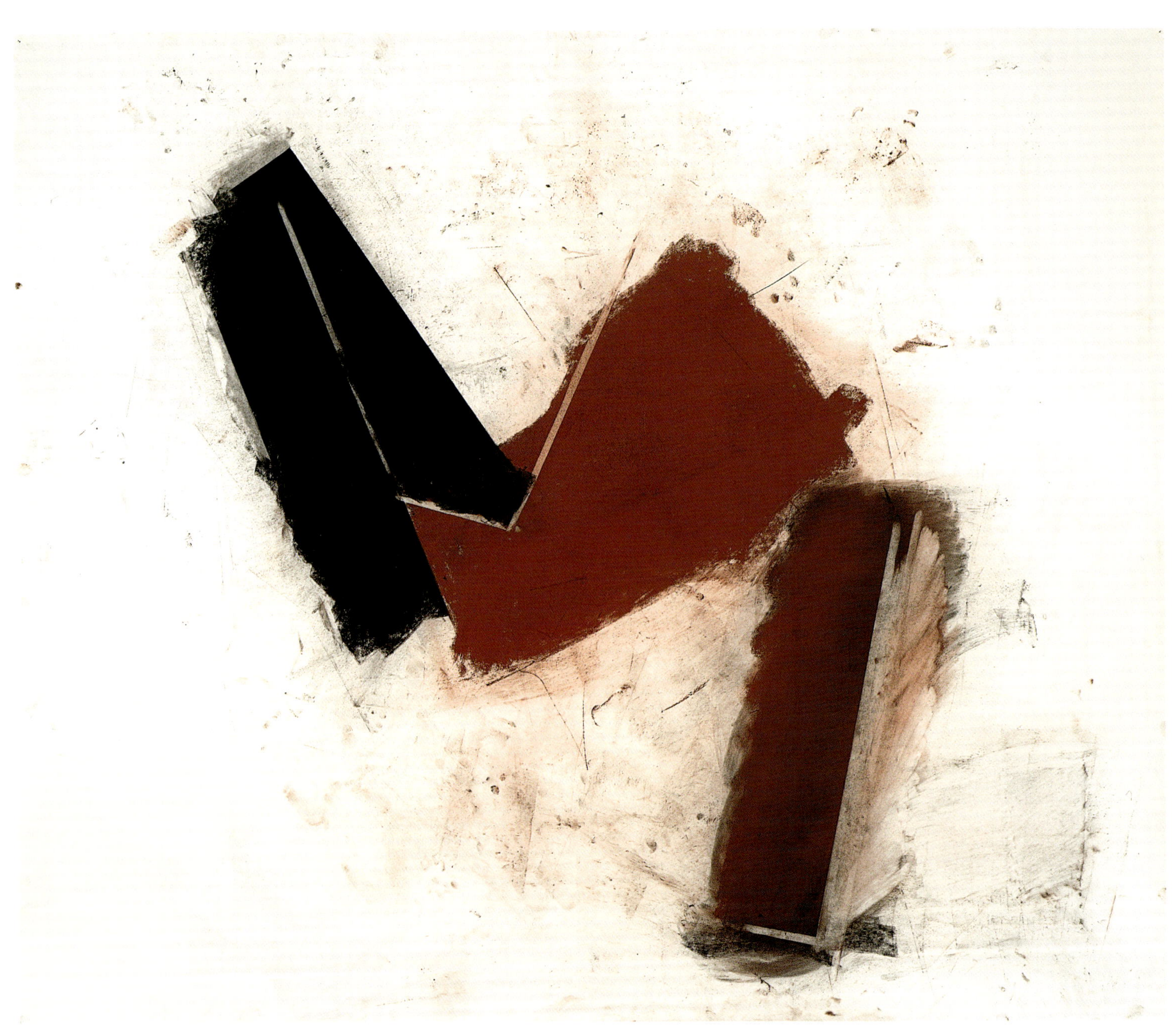

   untitled, 1994, chalk, charcoal and pastel on paper, 56 $\frac{1}{8}$ x 66"

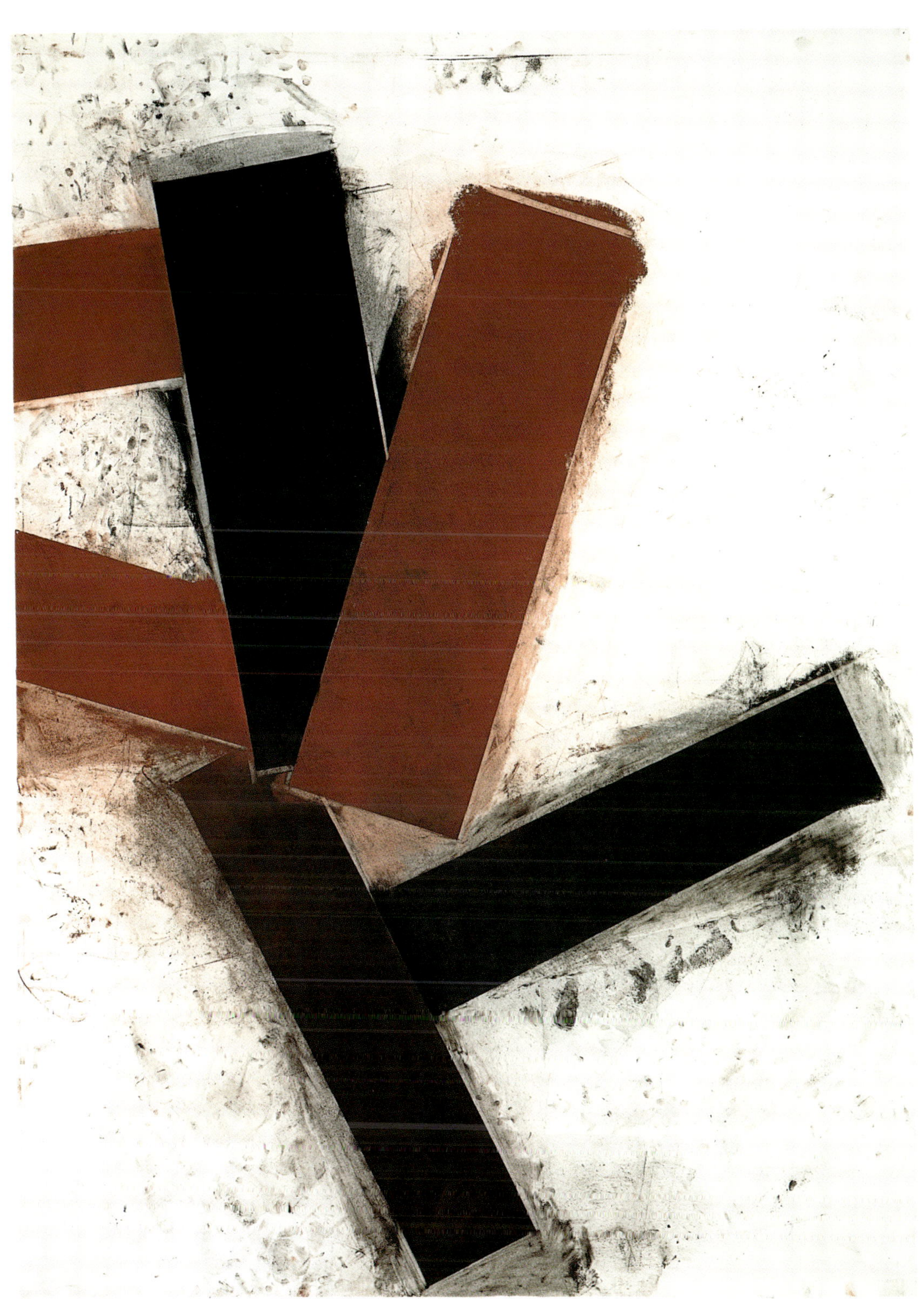

untitled, 1994, chalk, charcoal and pastel on paper, 72 x 52"

BIOGRAPHY

BORN

1941
New York, New York

EDUCATION

1964
New York University, B.A.

1965-67
Peace Corps in India

1969
New York University, M.A.

AWARDS

1975
Visual Arts Fellowship, Visual Arts Program,
National Endowment for the Arts

1984
Brandeis University Creative Arts Award

1986
Skowhegan Medal for Sculpture

1990
Award of Merit Medal for Sculpture, American Academy and
Institute of Arts and Letters, New York

1994
Elected to the Swedish Royal Academy of Fine Arts

SOLO EXHIBITIONS

1970
Paula Cooper Gallery, New York.

1972
Paula Cooper Gallery, New York.

1973
The Clocktower, Institute for Art and Urban Resources, New York.

1974
Paula Cooper Gallery, New York.
Galeria Salvatore Ala, Milan

1975
The Garage, London (with Jennifer Bartlett).
Walter Kelly Gallery, Chicago.
Paula Cooper Gallery, New York.

1976
Paula Cooper Gallery, Los Angeles.
Museum of Contemporary Art, Chicago.

1977
Max Protetch Gallery, Washington, D.C.
Albright-Knox Art Gallery, Buffalo, New York.
Susanne Hilberry Gallery, Birmingham, Michigan.
Paula Cooper Gallery, New York.
"Joel Shapiro: Drawings," Galerie Gillespie-de Laage, Paris.

1978
The Greenberg Gallery, St. Louis.
Galerie m, Bochum, Germany.

1979
Akron Art Institute, Ohio.
Paula Cooper Gallery, New York.
Galerie Gillespie-de Laage, Paris.
Ohio State University, Columbus.

1980
The Whitechapel Art Gallery, London. Traveled to Museum Haus
Lange, Krefeld, Germany; and Moderna Museet, Stockholm.

Galerie Mukai, Tokyo.

Asher/Faure, Los Angeles.

"Joel Shapiro: Lithographs, 1979-1980," Brooke Alexander
Gallery, New York. Traveled to Delahunty Gallery, Dallas.

Galerie Aronowitsch, Stockholm.

Paula Cooper Gallery, New York.

1980-81
Bell Gallery, Brown University, Providence. Traveled to
Georgia State University, Atlanta; and The Contemporary Arts
Center, Cincinnati.

1981
Ackland Art Museum, University of North Carolina, Chapel Hill.

John Stoller Gallery, Minneapolis.

Daniel Weinberg Gallery, San Francisco.

The Israel Museum, Jerusalem.

Galerie Mukai, Tokyo.

1981-82
Young-Hoffman Gallery, Chicago.

1982
"Joel Shapiro: Drawings," Paula Cooper Gallery, New York.

Portland Center of the Visual Arts, Portland, Oregon.

Susanne Hilberry Gallery, Birmingham, Michigan.

Yarlow/Salzman Gallery, Toronto.

1982-84
Whitney Museum of American Art, New York. Traveled to Dallas
Museum of Fine Arts, Dallas; Art Gallery of Ontario, Toronto;
and La Jolla Museum of Contemporary Art, La Jolla, California.

1983
Galerie Aronowitsch, Stockholm.

Paula Cooper Gallery, New York.

Asher/Faure, Los Angeles.

1984
"Joel Shapiro: Gouaches," Paula Cooper Gallery, New York.

Galerie Aronowitsch, Stockholm.

Paula Cooper Gallery, New York.

1985
Knoedler Kasmin, London.

1985-86
Stedelijk Museum, Amsterdam. Traveled to Kunstmuseum
Düsseldorf, Germany; and Staatliche Kunsthalle,
Baden-Baden, Germany.

1986
Seattle Art Museum.

Galerie Daniel Templon, Paris.

The John and Mable Ringling Museum of Arts, Sarasota, Florida.

Paula Cooper Gallery, New York.

Asher/Faure, Los Angeles.

Hal Bromm Gallery, New York.

1987
Donald Young Gallery, Chicago.

John Berggruen Gallery, San Francisco.

1987-88
"Joel Shapiro: Painted Wood," Hirshhorn Museum and
Sculpture Garden, Washington, D.C.

1988
Paula Cooper Gallery, New York.

Gallery Mukai, Tokyo.

Hans Strelow, Düsseldorf.

Susanne Hilberry Gallery, Birmingham, Michigan.

Galerie Daniel Templon, Paris.

"Joel Shapiro: Recent Sculptures and Drawings,"
Cleveland Museum of Art.

1989
Asher/Faure, Los Angeles.

"Playing with Human Geometry," Toledo Museum of Art, Ohio.

Paula Cooper Gallery, New York.

Colby College Museum of Art, Waterville, Maine.

Waddington Galleries, London.

1990
Pace Prints, New York.

The Greenberg Gallery, St. Louis, Missouri.

"Joel Shapiro Skulptur & Grafik 1985-1990," Museet i Varberg,
Varberg, Sweden.

Galerie Aronowitsch, Stockholm.

Paula Cooper Gallery, New York.

1990-91
"Joel Shapiro: Tracing the Figure," Baltimore Art Museum.
Traveled to Des Moines Art Center; and Center for the Fine
Arts, Miami.

Louisiana Museum of Modern Art, Humlebaek, Denmark.
Traveled to IVAM Centre Julio González, Valencia, Spain;
Kunsthalle Zürich; Musée des Beaux-Arts, Calais, France.

1991
Salon de Mars, Paris.

"Selected Drawings 1968-1990," Center for the Fine Arts, Miami.

Asher/Faure, Los Angeles.

Gallery Mukai, Tokyo.

John Berggruen Gallery, San Francisco.

1993
"Joel Shapiro: Sculpture and Drawings," The Pace Gallery, 32
East 57th Street, New York, and 142 Greene Street, New York.

1993-94
"Joel Shapiro: Skulpturen/Arbeiten auf Papier," Galerie
Karsten Greve, Cologne.

1994
"Joel Shapiro: Drawing & Sculpture," Gallery Seomi, Seoul.

1995
"Joel Shapiro: Teckningar," Galerie Aronowitsch,
Stockholm, Sweden.

Walker Art Center/Minneapolis Sculpture Garden May 15, 1995-
March 15, 1996 and The Nelson-Atkins Museum of Art/Kansas
City Sculpture Park, April 23-October 13, 1996.

PUBLIC COLLECTIONS

The Ackland Art Museum, Chapel Hill, North Carolina
Albright-Knox Art Gallery, Buffalo, New York
Art Gallery of Ontario, Toronto, Canada
Art Museum of South Texas, Corpus Christi, Texas
The Baltimore Museum of Art, Baltimore, Maryland
The British Museum, London, England
Brooklyn Museum, Brooklyn, New York
Cincinnati Art Museum, Cincinnati, Ohio
The Cleveland Museum of Art, Cleveland, Ohio
Colby College Museum of Art, Waterville, Maine
The Corcoran Gallery of Art, Washington, D.C.
Dallas Museum of Art, Dallas, Texas
The Denver Art Museum, Denver, Colorado
Des Moines Art Center, Des Moines, Iowa

The Detroit Institute of Arts, Detroit, Michigan

The Douglas S. Cramer Foundation, Los Angeles, California

Eli Broad Foundation, Los Angeles, California

Fogg Art Museum, Harvard University, Cambridge, Massachusetts

Grand Rapids Art Museum, Grand Rapids, Michigan

Hakone Open-Air Museum, Hakone-machi, Japan

Hall Family Foundation on permanent loan to
The Nelson-Atkins Museum of Art, Kansas City, Missouri

High Museum of Art, Atlanta, Georgia

Hirshhorn Museum and Sculpture Garden, Smithsonian
Institution, Washington, D.C.

Hood Museum of Art, Dartmouth College, Hanover,
New Hampshire

Israel Museum, Jerusalem, Israel

IVAM Centre Julio González, Valencia, Spain

John and Mable Ringling Museum, Sarasota, Florida

Kunsthaus Zürich, Zürich, Switzerland

Lannan Foundation, Los Angeles, California

Los Angeles County Museum of Art, Los Angeles, California

Louisiana Museum of Modern Art, Humlebaek, Denmark

The Menil Collection, Houston, Texas

The Metropolitan Museum of Art, New York, New York

Milwaukee Art Museum, Milwaukee, Wisconsin

Modern Art Museum of Fort Worth, Fort Worth, Texas

Moderna Museet, Stockholm, Sweden

Musée national d'art moderne, Centre Georges Pompidou,
Paris, France

The Museum of Contemporary Art, Los Angeles, California

Museum of Contemporary Art - San Diego, La Jolla, California

Museum of Fine Arts, Boston, Massachusetts

The Museum of Fine Arts, Houston, Texas

Museum of Modern Art, Friuli, Italy

The Museum of Modern Art, New York, New York

The Nasher Collection, Dallas, Texas

National Gallery of Art, Washington, D.C.

National Gallery of Australia, Canberra, Australia

The Newark Museum, Newark, New Jersey

North Carolina Museum of Art, Raleigh, North Carolina

Ohio State University, Columbus, Ohio

Parrish Art Museum, Southampton, New York

Philadelphia Museum of Art, Philadelphia, Pennsylvania

The Picker Art Gallery, Colgate University, Hamilton, New York

Rose Art Museum, Brandeis University, Waltham, Massachusetts

The Saint Louis Art Museum, Saint Louis, Missouri

Städtische Galerie im Lenbachhaus, Munich

Stedelijk Museum, Amsterdam, Netherlands

Tate Gallery, London, England

Tel Aviv Museum of Art, Tel Aviv, Israel

The Toledo Museum of Art, Toledo, Ohio

University of Massachusetts, Amherst, Massachusetts

University of Nebraska Art Galleries - Sheldon Memorial
Art Gallery, Lincoln, Nebraska

Walker Art Center, Minneapolis, Minnesota

Weatherspoon Art Gallery, University of North Carolina,
Greensboro, North Carolina

Whitney Museum of American Art, New York, New York

COMMISSIONS

1983-84
Cigna Corporation
Philadelphia, Pennsylvania
Architect: Kohn, Pederson, and Fox

1988
Fukuoka Sogo Bank
Fukuoka, Japan
Architect: Arata Isozaki

1988-89
Creative Artists Agency
Los Angeles, California
Architect: I.M. Pei and Partners

1988-89
Kawamura Memorial Museum of Art
Chiba, Japan
Architect: I. Ebihara

1988-90
Government Service Administration
Los Angeles, California
Architect: Ellerbe Becket

1989-90
Hood Museum of Art
Dartmouth College
Hanover, New Hampshire
Architect: Centerbrook, Charles Moore

1993
United States Holocaust Memorial Museum
Washington, D.C.
Architect: James Ingo Freed; Pei, Cobb, Freed & Partners

1994-95
Sony Plaza
New York City
Architect: Charles Gwathmey; Gwathmey & Siegel

1994-95
Friedrichstadt Passagen
Berlin, Germany
Architect: O.M. Ungers

LIST OF PLATES

PAINTED WOOD SCULPTURE

DRAWINGS

TEXT ILLUSTRATIONS

Cover:
untitled, 1994, oil paint on wood, 47 x 13 x 18½" (detail)

Photography:
Jerry L. Thompson, figure 1, p. 5
Geoffrey Clements, figure 2, p. 5
Ellen Page Wilson, pp. 10 and 15-53

Catalogue designed and produced by
Tomoko Makiura and Paul Pollard for PaceWildenstein

ISBN: 1-878283-49-9